Pathways of America
The Oregon Trail

by
Lynda Hatch

illustrated by Ted Warren

Cover by Ted Warren

Copyright © 1994, Good Apple

ISBN No. 0-86653-798-8

Printing No. 9876543

Good Apple
1204 Buchanan St., Box 299
Carthage, IL 62321-0299

Paramount Publishing

Table of Contents

Dedication

To my parents, Marley and Undine Sims, who instilled in me the desire to be a lifelong learner and to be curious about the world . . .

And to our family pioneers, Nathaniel Green McDonald and Rebecca Jane Munkers, who traveled by covered wagon to the Willamette Valley on the Oregon Trail in 1846.

Introduction

Pathways of America: The Oregon Trail covers the 2000-mile (3220-km) journey the emigrants faced as they traveled from the Missouri River to Oregon's Willamette Valley. Each of the major sites is highlighted in the order in which it would be encountered on the trip. The book includes detailed background information, emigrant journal quotations, stories that will be remembered by the students, and a bibliography. Quality activities for the students accompany each site to teach about life on the trail, natural and cultural information, geography concepts, and information about historic sites that can be visited. The activities are purposely designed in an open-ended manner, with few right and wrong answers, to allow students of all ages and abilities to ponder and tackle the problems.

The information is detailed to provide the teacher with a thorough, accurate background on the journey. Teachers usually don't have access to all the books that contain or the time to research the amount of detail that is needed for their teaching. Hopefully this book will provide that resource for the teacher. Although it is detailed, it will also be of interest to students, whether they read it on their own or they hear the stories read aloud to them. The book attempts to cover the information accurately. As with any history, there are often differing opinions, so numerous sources were used to get the most accepted information. Notice that when journals are quoted, the spelling and punctuation are left in their original forms.

As they study the Oregon Trail using the resources provided in this guide, your students will become fascinated by these amazing journeys, and they might even be inspired to seek adventures of their own, to enrich their own lives and contribute knowledge and understanding for all people.

Note: The term *Indian* has been used here as it was during pioneer days. Today, some people prefer the term *Indian*, some prefer *Native American*, and some feel either is fine. So as not to offend anyone, it is important to use the term that is most preferred in your area.

GA1473

Notes to the Teacher

Most activities in this book are open-ended with no particular right answers, as long as correct historical facts are used. With two of them the following information would help:

1. **Fort Boise Activity:** (page 54)
   A-Fisher, B-Mink, C-Marten, D-Muskrat, E-Raccoon, F-Beaver, G-River Otter, H-Weasel, I-Wolverine
   To help students with the colorations, this book is particularly good:
   The Audubon Society Field Guide to North American Mammals by John O. Whitaker, Jr. (New York, NY: Alfred A. Knopf, 1980).

2. **Oregon City Activity:** (page 89)
   Although this fictionalized region is shown as New Woodland, it is basically a map of the mouth of the Willamette River in Oregon, around Portland. Don't tell this to the students until the end of the activity. The Oregon Trail settlers built their town of Oregon City to the east of the "Mighty Waterfalls." It is interesting to see how often students also select this site for their settlement, not realizing of course that they are looking at a "real" map. At the end, tell the students the real names of these locations and compare their settlement choices. These are the real locations:

Big Rolling River	=	Columbia River
Swift River	=	Willamette River
Mt. Mason	=	Portland's Mt. Tabor
Mt. Scenic	=	Mt. Hood
Mighty Waterfalls	=	Oregon City's Willamette Falls
Forest Hills	=	Portland's West Hills
Glenwood Canyon	=	Route of Canyon Drive to Beaverton and Tualatin Valley
Sandy Island	=	Government Island
Rocky Island	=	Ross Island
Conifer National Forest	=	Mt. Hood National Forest
Green Valley	=	Willamette Valley

Note: In 1843, Asa Lovejoy and William Overton got in a canoe at Fort Vancouver to begin a trip upstream to Oregon City. About halfway along their 30-mile (48-km) trip, their Indian paddlers stopped the canoe on the west bank to rest. Overton decided this would be a good place to begin a settlement. But he didn't have the 25-cent filing fee for a land claim. Lovejoy paid the fee and received half of the claim, 320 acres (128 hectares) of what was to become downtown Portland. Overton grew restless and stayed only a few months. He bartered his half of the claim to Francis Pettygrove. When it was time to name the town, Pettygrove, from Maine, wanted the name Portland and Lovejoy, from Massachusetts, wanted Boston. A copper (coin) was flipped. Pettygrove won and the name became Portland! During the first years, Portland did not grow much. The emigrants were mainly farmers searching for rich valleys for farming rather than uncleared town lots. Portland began to grow when Captain John Couch arrived in 1846 and decided the deep-water site of Portland would be the head of navigation rather than the gravel-bound Oregon City. He sent out word that Portland was an international port. Daniel Lownsdale built a road which would become Canyon Drive to the Tualatin Valley where settlers were planting more and more wheat. Once gold was discovered in California in 1848, there was an instant market for Oregon's wheat, as well as lumber, fruit, and other farm products. With a road to get these crops to the port, Portland was on its way to becoming a city. Today, Oregon City is a suburb of Portland, rich in its early history of helping Oregon become a territory and a state.

Route of the Oregon Trail

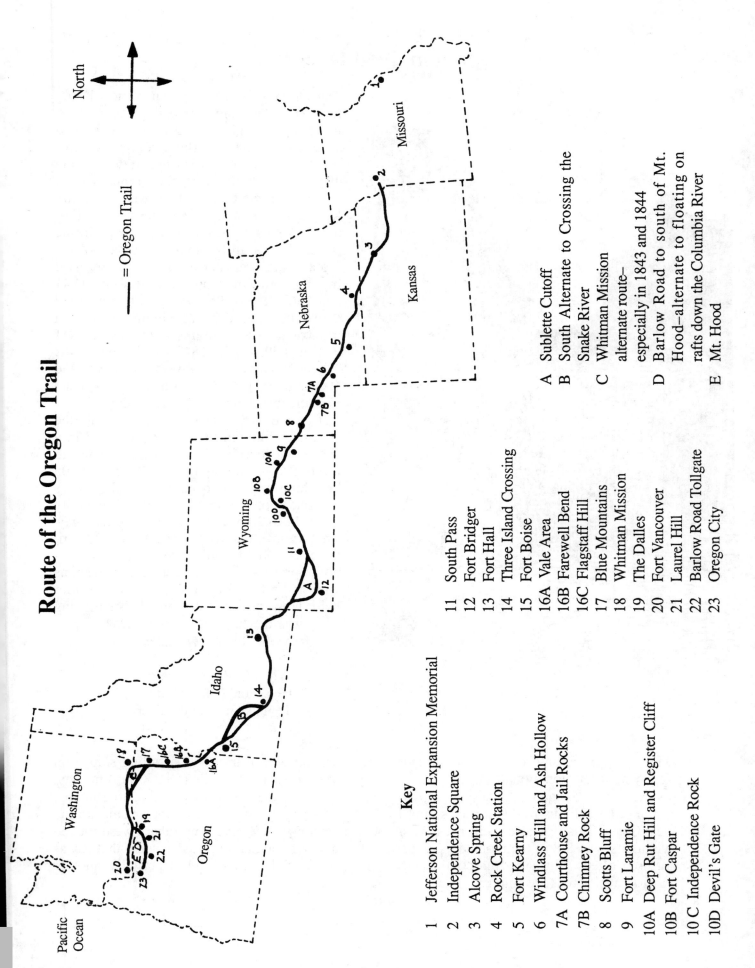

North

—— = Oregon Trail

Missouri

Kansas

Nebraska

Wyoming

Idaho

Washington

Oregon

Pacific Ocean

Key

1   Jefferson National Expansion Memorial
2   Independence Square
3   Alcove Spring
4   Rock Creek Station
5   Fort Kearny
6   Windlass Hill and Ash Hollow
7A   Courthouse and Jail Rocks
7B   Chimney Rock
8   Scotts Bluff
9   Fort Laramie
10A Deep Rut Hill and Register Cliff
10B Fort Caspar
10 C Independence Rock
10D Devil's Gate

11   South Pass
12   Fort Bridger
13   Fort Hall
14   Three Island Crossing
15   Fort Boise
16A Vale Area
16B Farewell Bend
16C Flagstaff Hill
17   Blue Mountains
18   Whitman Mission
19   The Dalles
20   Fort Vancouver
21   Laurel Hill
22   Barlow Road Tollgate
23   Oregon City

A   Sublette Cutoff
B   South Alternate to Crossing the Snake River
C   Whitman Mission alternate route—especially in 1843 and 1844
D   Barlow Road to south of Mt. Hood—alternate to floating on rafts down the Columbia River
E   Mt. Hood

GA1473

Oregon Trail Overview

The Oregon Trail was given National Historic Trail designation by Congress in 1978, honoring this great migration that helped assure that one day the Oregon Country would be part of the United States. In the early years of the trail, the pioneers were truly emigrants because they were officially leaving their country, the United States. Pioneer journals often referred to "back in the States." The trail began as a footpath of the Indians and was later used by explorers, fur trappers, and missionaries. Between 1841 and 1869 at least 350,000 people emigrated along the trail. The first significant wagon train of families moving West was in 1841 with just 32 people. 1843 was known as the "Great Migration" because between 875 and 1000 emigrants, 120 wagons and 5000 head of cattle traveled the Oregon Trail. One traveler on the trail in 1852, a big year, said the column (although they rarely traveled in a single-file line), from the earliest wagon to the last to get through, was 500 miles (805 km) long and would take a month to pass any one spot! They were able to travel only about 12 to 20 miles (19 to 32 km) each day. This approximately 2000-mile (3220-km) trip was difficult and dangerous across unfamiliar prairies, deserts, rivers, and mountains with just a few forts along the way to offer help. However, it just seemed like moving West was the thing to do. One Dakota pioneer from the Red River Valley wrote:

> When God made man
> He seemed to think it best
> To make him in the East,
> And let him travel West.

One option of getting to the West without going over land was to travel on a sailing ship from New York or Boston around Cape Horn. This was a six-month, 13,000-mile (20,930-km) trip that was also very dangerous. They could save three months of the voyage by sailing to Panama, crossing the isthmus by boat, mules, and by foot, and then trying to catch another ship up the West Coast. This was also dangerous. Many people caught yellow fever and others were robbed by bandits who hid in the mountains. Crossing Panama was such an unpleasant route that it was not used often. When the transcontinental railroad was completed in 1869, it provided another way to travel across the country.

2

GA1473

For all the hardships and sacrifices, there were many reasons the emigrants caught the "Oregon Fever" and left their old lives behind, starting on bold adventures in a new land.

1. There were economic depressions in 1837 and again in 1842. Since there was no welfare or unemployment insurance, the lure of free land and a chance to start a new life were appealing. Pioneers believed that the Donation Land Act would be extended to include Oregon, and it *was* passed by Congress in 1850. That meant that every white American male over the age of eighteen could have 320 acres (128 hectares) of land if he had lived on it for the four years before December 1850. His wife was allowed to claim the same amount of land in her own name. That meant that families could have 640 acres (256 hectares) of free land! The Donation Land Act also said that anyone who had settled in Oregon from 1851 to 1855 could claim about half as much as the earlier settlers if they agreed to farm it. Even though they were attracted by free land, the emigrants could not have been poor. It cost from $700 to $1500 to outfit a family for the trip. The U.S. government was offering free land to encourage people to move West. Many people believed that the United States should stretch from the Atlantic to the Pacific coasts. This feeling that the United States was meant to rule all the land between the oceans became known as Manifest Destiny. At first, both England and the United States claimed the Oregon Country. Many Americans felt that if they settled there in large numbers, their claim to the land would be strengthened. This, of course, did not consider the rights and feelings of the Indians.

2. Other people left the Mississippi Valley hoping to escape the many diseases that were especially common in the swampy, lowland areas such as malaria, cholera, scarlet fever, typhoid, dysentery, tuberculosis, and yellow fever. These diseases, however, were also found along parts of the trail, especially amid unsanitary conditions.

3. Amazing claims were being made about the Oregon Country, and people in the East believed what was often propaganda. One group of emigrants was told, as they were starting on their journey, that Oregon was a "pioneer's paradise" where "the pigs are running about under the great acorn trees, round and fat, and already cooked, with knives and forks sticking in them so that you can cut off a slice whenever you are hungry." One emigrant, Dr. White, had written home, "Friends, you are traveling to the garden of Eden, a land flowing with milk and honey, and just let me tell you, the clover grows wild all over Oregon, and when you wade through it, it reaches your chin." They heard the trip West would not be difficult, which, of course, was not true. The route was even described as being "easy, safe, and expeditious." Many read detailed descriptions in emigrant guidebooks written by John Charles Fremont (and others) who had explored and mapped much of the West. Their sense of adventure and their feeling of restlessness urged them to go. They read editorials in newspapers about the West and read letters from their friends and relatives who were now in Oregon. They felt that if their neighbor had been able to make it, they could too.

4. Some went for an improved climate. They were tired of cold, icy winters and hot, humid summers. Western Oregon had fairly warm but rainy winters and comfortable summers. One piece of propaganda about Oregon said, very inaccurately, that the "soil of the valley is rich beyond comparison . . . rain rarely falls, even in the winter season; but the dews are sufficiently heavy to compensate for its absence."

5. Some of the emigrants went West so they could practice their religion as they wished. This was particularly true of the Mormons who moved to Utah, hoping to leave religious persecution.

GA1473

6. Some people left the East because, for either humanitarian or economic reasons, they were bothered by the existence of slavery.

7. After the Civil War, many people left because their homes had been devastated and they wanted a fresh start to their lives.

8. Farmers in the Mississippi Valley and the plains states had begun to feel crowded. Some were concerned because their neighbors were as close as twelve miles (19 km) away! It was time to move West!

As you read about the Oregon Trail, remember that you will find many differing opinions on almost everything about the trail. Was the trail 2000 or 2200 miles (3220 or 3542 km) long? Did emigrants ever ride in the wagons? How often were they attacked by Indians (and vice versa)? Did they use only oxen to pull the wagons? The list could go on and on. Looking at the varying reasons people went West in the first place shows that there would probably have been different approaches to life on the trail. Consider them *all*, avoiding stereotypes and Hollywood portrayals, and you will have a richer appreciation and understanding of this time in American history.

GA1473

Before You Begin

If the definitions for the following words are clear, the concepts in this book will be easier. Reading history can be difficult because of words that aren't in use today. Students will enjoy the spellings and word usages of the pioneer journal quotations. The text in this guide was written as background information for the teacher and for the students. Depending on individual abilities, teachers may need to guide students through the reading.

adobe
anniversary
archaeology
art–impressionism
art–modern
art–realism
artifacts
auger
blacksmith
bullwhacker
caulk
chisel
cholera
Christianity
converting
cooper
cut and wrought nails
descent/ascent
desolate
Donation Land Act
dysentery
economic depression
edit
editorials
emigrant/immigrant
epidemics
epitaphs
erosion
excavation
expedition
extinction
felt (cloth)
fording (a river)
49th parallel
generations
geology

glade
goods
gulch
horde
Hudson's Bay Company
inaugural address
infantry
in vain
Jew's harp
judicial court
keg
knead
lard
laundress
Lewis and Clark
Louisiana Purchase
Manifest Destiny
massacre
medallion
militia
mired
monotony
Mormons
mountain men/fur trade
mouth (of river)
nomadic
oasis
pact
paltry
pelt
peril
petition
pilgrimage
portage
post/fort
prairie

prairie schooner
provisions
ransom
replica
resistance (to disease)
ruts
scripture
sculpture
sediment
sesquicentennial
slough
smallpox
solidify
stagecoach
stampede
steep grade
stockaded fort
survey (measuring)
swale
switch (for beating)
tanner
teamster
telegraph
tipi
toll
trading post
tragedy
transcontinental
voyageur
wagon axle
wheelwright
whetstone
widow
yellow fever
yeomen
yoke

Note:

Pioneer: borrowed from the French *pionnier*, a derivation of the Old French *paonier*. The form originally denoted a foot soldier sent ahead to clear the way. This was a derivation of *paon*, a foot soldier. Today, *pioneer* means "a person or group that explores new areas of thought or activity." Pioneers begin or take part in the development of something new and go first to prepare the way for others.

GA1473

Jefferson National Expansion Memorial

Downtown St. Louis, Missouri
Near the west bank of the Mississippi River
St. Louis County

The Jefferson National Expansion Memorial is a park created in memory of Thomas Jefferson and the many pioneers who explored and settled the West, from the Mississippi River to the Pacific Ocean, between 1803 and 1890. A life-sized bronze statue of Jefferson is at the entrance to the Memorial's Museum of Westward Expansion.

Thomas Jefferson had a vision of a United States that would stretch across the continent. In 1803, Jefferson succeeded in buying lands the French had owned. This "Louisiana Purchase" included lands west of the Mississippi River and east of the Rocky Mountains. It cost the U.S. twenty-three million dollars, about fifteen cents an acre, and doubled the size of our young country. When Jefferson purchased the land, most people didn't know exactly what the United States had bought.

In 1804, Jefferson sent Meriwether Lewis and William Clark to survey these new lands. They were also to observe, collect, measure, and write about these unknown lands west of St. Louis. Jefferson's instructions to Lewis were: "The object of your mission is to explore the Missouri river, and such principal stream of it, as, by its course and communication with the waters of the Pacific Ocean . . . may offer the most direct and practicable water communication across this continent, for the purpose of commerce." When Lewis and Clark finally returned two years later, their official reports excited people about the West, and exploration started, especially among fur trappers.

At the Museum of Westward Expansion visitors are shown what it was like to go West in the nineteenth century through exhibits, films, and artifacts. It shows the way people lived, what they ate, what they said, and even the music they heard. The museum is located underground beneath the famous Gateway Arch. This is a soaring 630-foot (191.1-m) stainless steel arch symbolizing St. Louis' historic role as a gateway for westward expansion. The arch is known among engineers as an "inverted, weighted catenary curve." A catenary curve is the shape made by a chain hanging freely between two points of support. Trams carry visitors to the observation area inside the top of the arch, giving a spectacular view of St. Louis and the Mississippi River.

GA1473

Although there were already many trails to the West, including Indian trails, the route of the explorations of Lewis and Clark, and the trails of the fur trappers and missionaries, the following is a brief description of some of the later trails:

1. **The Oregon Trail:** Missouri River to Oregon's Willamette Valley
2. **The Santa Fe Trail:** Missouri River to Santa Fe, New Mexico
3. **The California Trail:** Followed the Oregon Trail until it branched off to California
4. **The Mormon Trail:** Closely followed the Oregon Trail until it branched to Utah
5. **The Boseman Trail:** Branched north from the Oregon Trail to Virginia City, Montana
6. **The Gila Trail:** Santa Fe, New Mexico, to San Diego, California

The Jefferson National Expansion Memorial was built to honor the vision of President Thomas Jefferson and the courage and determination of the settlers and Indians of the West. From time to time throughout history, anniversaries and monuments have been created to honor special events. For example, in 1930 President Herbert Hoover proclaimed the Covered-Wagon Centennial, marking the 100th anniversary of the first wagon crossing from St. Louis to the Rocky Mountains. The sesquicentennial (150th anniversary) of the Oregon Trail was celebrated in 1993.

Sesquicentennial Logo

Jefferson National Expansion Memorial Activity

Below you will find examples of items designed for the 150th anniversary of the Oregon Trail. After looking at these items, design some of your own to mark an anniversary or honor the Oregon Trail.

Commemorative Postage Stamp   **Pendleton Blanket**   **Medallion**

1. **Official Sesquicentennial Logo:**
   This logo can be found on any article that officially represented the Oregon Trail Sesquicentennial.

2. **Oregon Trail Commemorative Postage Stamp:**
   The process for obtaining a commemorative stamp is very involved and competitive. The U.S. Postal Service receives 30,000 stamp proposals each year but only 30 are selected. This stamp was designed to remind the nation of the Oregon Trail and its significance to the development of the United States.

3. **Pendleton Commemorative Oregon Trail Indian Blanket:**
   Oregon's Pendleton Woolen Mills are famous for their many years of making fine woolen products including Indian blankets. Only 500 special Oregon Trail blankets were made with the profits going to the Oregon Trail Celebration. The design symbolized, in sunrise colors, the journey from the East across the earth-toned plains to the green, fertile valley and forests, and the blue Pacific of the West Coast. Blanket 1 was presented to former First Lady Barbara Bush in 1991.

4. **Oregon Trail Medallion:**
   These special Oregon Trail commemorative medallions were authorized by the Oregon Legislature. The profits support historic sites and observances in state parks. The medallions show the strength of mind and body of the early settlers as they made their way West.

Independence Square

Spider Skillet

Liberty and Lexington Streets
Downtown Independence, MO
Jackson County

If the Oregon Trail had an official starting point, it was the Courthouse Square in Independence. Historian Francis Parkman described the town in 1846. "A multitude of shops had sprung up to furnish the emigrants . . . with necessaries for their journey and there was an incessant hammering and banging from a dozen blacksmith's sheds, where the heavy wagons were being repaired, and the horses and oxen shod." Independence was one of the "jumping-off points" on the Missouri River where pioneers gathered to start the trip. It was important for pioneers to begin their travels between April 15 and May 15 of each season. If they left early in the spring, they could be sure that the prairie grass would be high and green for the animals to feed. A late start could mean disaster, especially if an early snow blocked the mountain passes. In the beginning, Independence was the best known jumping-off point, but soon cities such as St. Joseph, Council Bluffs, and Westport were also places where pioneers purchased wagons, livestock, and provisions for their journey, if they hadn't brought these supplies with them.

GA1473

A covered wagon body averaged 10' long, 4' wide, 2' deep (3.04 m long, 1.22 m wide, .61 m deep) and would hold up to 2500 pounds (1125 kg). This was not a lot considering they had to take whatever they would need for a 2000-mile (3220-km) trip which would take five or six months. They also took whatever they would need to start a new home and job in Oregon. Often, however, they overpacked. Pioneer A.J. McCall wrote, "They laid in an over-supply of bacon, flour and beans, and in addition thereto every . . . useless article that the wildest fancy could devise or human ingenuity could invent . . . ." If a large family could afford to do so, it took two or three wagons.

Some pioneers traveled in farm wagons they had converted for trail travel and some bought wagons specifically built for this journey. Most wagons were painted blue and had red wheels. From a distance, the wagons looked like small ships sailing across the plains so they were often called "prairie schooners." These were not the large wagons that are sometimes mistakenly shown in pictures. Large Conestoga wagons were used for hauling commercial freight and would have been too heavy to make it over the mountains of the Oregon Trail. A wagon had to be strong enough not to break down under the heavy load yet light enough not to place too much strain on the oxen. As oxen became weakened during the trip, the load often had to be lightened. Anything not necessary for survival was thrown out along the trail.

OX YOKE

To pull the wagons, pairs of oxen were put in wooden harnesses called yokes. Emigrants were encouraged to take three or four yoke of oxen for each wagon. Although two yoke of oxen could pull the wagon, three yoke eased the work and lessened the risk of eventual exhaustion. Some pioneers preferred horses or mules, but oxen were more durable and dependable for the long

10

GA1473

journey. Oxen sold for less and one ox could pull as much as two mules. They endured the heat and fatigue better and were less likely to stampede or be stolen by Indians. These oxen became like members of the family. A man drove oxen by walking beside them, cracking a long bullwhip. Mules were faster, stayed fat on poor feed, and had stronger hooves. A man with mules used reins and had to sit in the bouncy wagon hour after hour staying alert because mules were sulky and sometimes got scared, even of their own shadows, and ran wildly away. Most people agreed that horses that pulled wagons could not survive the trip eating dry prairie grasses. Each family usually had several riding horses for scouting and hunting. Occasionally cows traveled the trail to provide milk and meat. Milk could be placed in a bucket tied to the wagon, and the bouncing of the wagons turned it into butter by the end of the day!

Emigrants studied guidebooks to decide what to pack in their wagons. To get ready for the start of the trip, the pioneers bought whatever they still needed for the trip. At the jumping-off points, cows, horses, sheep, goats, and chickens were sold to the highest bidders. The packing list consisted mostly of food, chosen by what would stay fresh. For example, thick slabs of smoked bacon would keep as long as they were protected from the heat of the plains. Packing bacon in a barrel of bran was one way of insulating the meat. Coffee was for adults, children, and even animals. It disguised the taste of the bitter, alkali-filled water so effectively that a horse that refused to drink water was convinced to drink coffee instead. Personal items were packed in large trunks.

Independence Square Activity

Below is a suggested supply list for a wagon trip to Oregon. This list, typical of many such lists, recommended that over half of the 2500-pound (1125-kg) load be made of food. The prices listed varied greatly, and inflation was an economic problem then too. Only one year after this list was made, prices went up 50 percent, bringing the total close to $900.

Let's pretend you're a pioneer traveling to Oregon with a spouse and two children. You've had a hard year and don't have the $570.85 that the following recommended supplies would cost. On another paper, list what you would choose to take if you had only $400 to spend. You might have to research what some of these items are. After you make your list, write a paragraph explaining why you chose (and did not choose) the items you did. Be sure your supplies total no more than $400.

Suggested Supplies for Crossing the Oregon Trail

3 yoke of oxen, $75 per yoke	$225.00	1 skillet	$1.50
1 wagon and cover	100.00	2 water buckets	.50
1 tent	15.00	2 small tin pails	1.00
12 sacks of flour	36.00	75 feet (23 m) of rope	2.50
400 pounds (180 kg) of bacon	40.00	6 tablespoons	.50
100 pounds (45 kg) of coffee	30.00	2 camp kettles	1.25
40 pounds (18 kg) of candles	10.00	4 gold pans	3.00
10 pounds (4.5 kg) of tea	10.00	4 picks	5.00
Yeast powders	5.00	4 shovels	5.00
50 pounds (22.5 kg) of salt	1.00	2 axes	2.50
3 pounds (1.35 kg) of pepper	.50	2 bread pans	1.00
2 bushels (70 liters) of beans	3.00	1 wagon bucket	1.00
15 gallons (57 liters) of vinegar	4.00	1 each, handsaw and drawing knife	2.00
25 pounds (11 kg) of bar soap	3.00	1 pair of gold scales	4.00
50 pounds (23 kg) of lard	5.00	2 chisels and augers	2.00
1 gross matches	1.00	2 files	.50
1 ten-gallon (38-liter) water keg	1.25	1 each, hatchet and hammer	1.00
1 coffee mill	.75	2 gimlets	.25
2 coffee pots	1.50	10 pounds (5 kg) of cut and wrought nails	.75
8 tin plates	.50	1 whetstone	.10
8 tin cups	.50	4 bushels (141 liters) dried apples	6.00
2 frying pans	1.00	1 bushel (35 liters) dried peaches	2.00
4 butcher knives	2.00	50 pounds (23 kg) of rice	5.00
6 knives and 6 forks	1.50	200 pounds (90 kg) of sugar	25.00

Alcove Spring: Early Days on the Trail

The beginning days of the Oregon Trail journey usually started with struggles to develop a travel routine. The journals tell that the pioneers often lost animals and had problems "hitching up" the oxen and learning how to use their equipment. It was fortunate that as they were getting used to traveling, the trail itself was fairly easy. Sleeping outside was an exciting adventure at first, but later in the trip exhaustion would put them to sleep in seconds. At the beginning, the emigrants for the Oregon Trail and the Santa Fe Trail followed the same route until the trails split near today's Gardner, Kansas. The Oregon Trail travelers then passed through wooded groves and tall grasslands, among lovely wildflowers and around small hills. They crossed the Wakarusa, Kansas, Red Vermillion, and Black Vermillion Rivers.

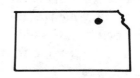

7 miles (11 km) south of Marysville, KS
Marshall County

On the east side of the Big Blue River was a lovely wooded glade called Alcove Spring that was a popular camping spot for the emigrants. Here a stream of cool, clear water fell over a rock ledge to a pool ten feet (3.04 m) below. The area was heavily timbered with oak, cottonwood, walnut, and sycamore trees. In the spring when the pioneers arrived, wildflowers bloomed everywhere and tall grasses were lush and plentiful. Mosquitoes could be a problem, though. Joe Meek joked that other emigrants "lied," that the mosquitoes really weren't as large as turkeys. He said the biggest one he saw was no larger than a crow!

Edwin Bryant of the ill-fated Donner party named Alcove Spring, and George M. McKinstry carved the name in 8-inch (20.32-cm) high letters on a large flat stone. Bryant wrote on May 26th, 1846, "We continued to ascend elevated ridges until we reached the bluffs which overlook the Big Blue River. Descending from these, and ascertaining that from the late rains the stream was so much swollen as not to be fordable, we encamped on a slope of the prairie . . . . In the banks and bed of this small stream are several springs of delicious cold water." He continued on May 27th, "About three-fourths of a mile from our camp we found a large spring of water, as cold and pure as if it had just been melted from ice. It gushes from a ledge of rocks . . . . The whole is buried in a variety of shrubbery . . . we named this 'Alcove Spring.'"

Emigrants often had to camp for days at Alcove Spring, waiting for the Big Blue River to lower so it could be crossed safely. John Minto wrote in 1844 that he found the Big Blue a "raging torrent . . . with whirlpools." Usually the wagons forded (or "swam") across, but when the water was high, pioneers had to wait or build rafts. It was during this kind of wait that members of the Donner group named this site Alcove Spring. Tragedy in the Sierra Mountains on their way to California later made the Donner party famous. When snow trapped the wagon train, the people dug in to wait for spring. Nearly half of the party of eighty-seven died and the survivors resorted to eating the dead. Here, at Alcove Spring, seventy-year-old Sarah Keyes died. She had been in failing health but refused to be left behind. She was buried beneath a large oak on a small hill above the spring near where a monument now stands. A lock of her grandma's gray hair was cut for eight-year-old Patty by her father, James Reed. This hair was later found clutched in Patty's hand when she was rescued from a snow cave in the Sierra Mountains in March 1847.

Although the emigrants were struggling with developing a travel routine during the beginning days on the Oregon Trail, it was also a time of fairly easy travel. They had the excitement and energy of recreational times in the evenings of singing, square dancing, and playing musical instruments such as the fiddle, banjo, flute, guitar, Jew's harp, and hammered dulcimer. Sometimes wagon trains stopped to rest on Sundays where there was time for religious sermons, recreation, and chores—washing clothes, making repairs on the wagons, and cooking. Many emigrants soon decided that it was so far to travel to Oregon that they must move on every day, not resting on Sundays. They didn't want to get caught in the winter snows in the western mountains. However, some historians believe that the wagon trains that did stop on Sundays made it to Oregon as quickly and in better shape because they *did* allow regular time for rest and repairs.

One of the best accounts of daily life on the trail was written by pioneer Jesse Applegate, captain of several hundred pioneers with a large group of cattle and horses. He wrote "A Day with the Cow Column in 1843," describing an eighteen-hour day. The following is a part of that account that describes the evening routine, including recreational time: "Everyone is busy preparing fires of buffalo chips to cook the evening meal, pitching tents and otherwise preparing for the night. There are anxious watchers for the absent wagon. But as the sun goes down it rolls into camp, the bright, speaking face of the doctor (Whitman) declares without words that both mother and child are well. It is not yet eight o'clock when the first watch is to be set; the evening meal is just over. Near the river a violin makes lively music, and some youths improvise a dance; in another quarter a flute whispers its lamet to the deepening night. It has been a prosperous day; more than 20 miles have been accomplished . . . ."

Spider Skillet

Alcove Spring Activity

Write a poem or song that tells about life on the Oregon Trail.
You might want to write about the early days of the trail such as:
- The lush prairie grasses and wildflowers
- Fording or ferrying across the rivers
- Choosing a wagon train captain
- Choosing supplies and loading the wagon
- New animals–oxen, mules, horses, cows, dogs
- New friends from other wagons
- Evenings of singing, dancing, and playing musical instruments
- Getting used to long days of travel and walking beside the wagons
- Helping with the meals by hunting for food and firewood or by cooking

If you choose to write a song, you may wish to write new words to a familiar tune. It would be nice to use a tune that was popular during pioneer times such as "Oh Susanna" by Stephen Foster. You could also use tunes from familiar spirituals. With a little research, you can find many more songs of the pioneer days.

If you choose to write a poem, you may use any style of poetry that you wish. It can be a poem that rhymes or does not rhyme. You may wish to write a cinquain poem. This is a poem that contains five lines. There are several different patterns such as:

lst line: noun (title)
2nd line: two descriptive words
3rd line: three action words
4th line: four words to express feelings
5th line: one-word synonym for title

16

GA1473

Rock Creek Station

6 miles (10 km) SE of Fairbury, NE
Jefferson County

Rock Creek Station was the site of a Pony Express station, was on the Oregon Trail route, and was known for the historic McCanles-Hickok gunfight. The trail past Rock Creek had been used for many years by Indians, trappers, and traders. By the 1840s it had become a well-used campsite on the Oregon Trail. Although the stream crossing was difficult due to steep, sloping banks, Rock Creek had all the necessities for the early-day travelers–good spring water, wood for fires, and grass for grazing.

David McCanles settled at Rock Creek Station in 1859. He decided he could earn money by making the creek crossing easier for emigrants. He built a toll bridge across the creek for the many travelers through the area. The Overland Stage, which carried the mail and the wealthier passengers, changed horses here while riders had refreshments. There were freighters, wagon trains, and almost every type of traveler.

In 1860 the Pony Express came through Rock Creek Station. It became Nebraska Station Number Two, one of about 130 such stations on the 2000-mile (3220-km) route from St. Joseph to Sacramento. McCanles leased property to the Pony Express, and Horace Wellman was placed in charge.

In the spring of 1861, 23-year-old James Hickok was sent to Rock Creek Station as a stable hand, caring for the stock. When McCanles and Wellman had an argument over the lease money that was owed for the Pony Express station, Hickok became involved in the argument and shot and killed McCanles. There are many theories of why Hickok killed him, but regardless of the motives behind this murder, it marked the beginning of Hickok's bloody career as a gunfighter. By the time of his death at the age of 39, James Butler "Wild Bill" Hickok had killed at least three dozen men, plus others in wars and Indian battles. Hickok himself said he killed about two hundred people. Rock Creek Station was important for being on the route West, but this famous gunfight made the site well-known. Today, Rock Creek Station is open to the public as a visitor center, protecting this historic area.

GA1473

Rock Creek Station

18

The Pony Express Story

Before 1860 the mail routes from the Eastern United States to California were not very reliable. There wasn't an official mail service. Mail went on ships to Panama and was carried across the tropical jungles and then reloaded on a west coast ship, taking about twenty-two days. Mail also went on an overland stagecoach route that took about twenty-five days. William H. Russell of the freighting firm Russell, Majors, & Waddell believed mail should have its own service that could guarantee delivery. He developed the Pony Express and boasted that it could get mail from St. Joseph, Missouri, to Sacramento, California, faster than any other company. He hoped that the Pony Express would solve the mail delivery problem until the telegraph lines could be completed.

The Pony Express lasted only sixteen months before the transcontinental telegraph put it out of service. The founders were heavily in debt and lost $100,000. The fees charged for carrying the mail did not cover the cost of running the service. At $5.00 for each ½ ounce (14.17 gr), some of the letters cost over $25.00 to mail. However, with 500 horses, 200 men at the stations to care for them, and huge amounts of grain that had to be brought in at 10 to 25 cents a pound, the expenses were too great.

Pony Express

With the Pony Express, the mail took about ten days to cover 1996 miles (3214 km). It was carried by about 120 courageous young riders who faced such dangers as bandits, hostile Indians, blizzards, raging rivers, and hot deserts. The rider would gallop up to a relay station along the route, throw his mail pouch onto a waiting horse, and be off, all within two minutes. These relay stations were about ten miles (16 km) apart and were usually located at a stream or spring. About every fifty miles (80 km) was a "home" station where the riders could sleep. The record run over the whole line was made carrying President Abraham Lincoln's Inaugural Address in seven days and seventeen hours.

The riders were selected from the most hardy and courageous of the frontiersmen. They had to be lightweight, tough enough to ride through storms and over snowcapped mountains, across burning deserts, and through streams. They agreed not to use profane language, not to get drunk, not to gamble, not to treat animals cruelly, and not to do anything else that was incompatible with the conduct of a gentleman. Each rider was given a small Bible to carry among his belongings.

Rock Creek Station Activity

An advertisement recruiting Pony Express riders in March, 1860, in San Francisco, California, said:

Now, imagine how a wagon train captain was chosen among the pioneers. Wagon train captains were chosen from their past experiences on the trail and for their leadership qualities, not from advertisement posters. However, imagine there *had* been posters seeking wagon train captains. Design such a poster with words and illustrations showing that you know what life was like on the Oregon Trail.

GA1473

Fort Kearny
1848-1871

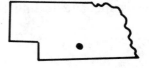

State Historical Park
7 miles (11 km) SE of Kearney, NE
Kearney County

With the increase of overland emigration to Oregon after 1842, a series of military forts were established to protect travelers from their fear of the Indians. One of these was Fort Kearny, established in 1848. It was built in a square shape out of wood, sod, and adobe. The buildings and cottonwood trees surrounded a parade ground. It started as an open fort and was not stockaded until later. Fort Kearny was known as an unhealthy and uncomfortable post. Snakes slithered through sod walls and into the beds of soldiers. Although misspelled, it was named for Colonel Stephen Watts Kearney who had explored the area in 1838.

The pioneers had started their Oregon Trail journey from several towns, known as "jumping-off points," such as Independence. Just east of the fort, all of the trails merged, so by Fort Kearny, the emigrants were all heading west together. However, most Mormon emigrants followed the north side of the Platte River and the non-Mormons traveled south of the Platte.

Fort Kearny was constructed on the south side of the Platte River. Although the emigrants followed it for much of their journey, the Platte was often a disappointment. It was wide and shallow (3 to 6 feet [.9 to 1.82 m] deep), difficult to cross, unpleasant to drink, and too muddy for washing. Emigrants described it as "a moving mass of pure sand," "flowed bottom side up," and "too thick to drink and too thin to plow." On May 27, 1852, Lodisa Frizzell wrote: "Two horsemen were testing the route setting willow poles deeply in the sand bars to mark the way . . . wagons . . . were two hours in crossing." John C. Fremont wrote on July 2, 1842: ". . . exception of the few dry bars, the bed of the river is generally quicksands, in which the carts begin to sink rapidly so soon as the mules halted . . ."

GA147

Fort Kearny quickly developed into one of the most important stops on the Oregon Trail. Emigrants often stopped at the fort to shoe horses or oxen, repair wagons, or send a letter home. On June 2, 1849, Lieutenant Woodbury, founder of the fort, wrote, "The post is at present very poorly prepared to give to the emigrants the assistance which very many have required even at this point so near the beginning of their journey."

As the fort grew over the years, better facilities were developed to help the emigrants. The fort's main purpose was to supply forts further west that were guarding the eastern end of the Oregon Trail. However, the commanding officer was allowed to sell supplies "at cost" (without a profit) to emigrants needing them. Often supplies were given freely to pioneers facing emergencies. Beginning in 1850, the fort had once-a-month mail and passenger service on the stagecoach. It was also a stop on the Pony Express route.

After 1854 hostility among the Plains Indian tribes, particularly the Cheyenne and Sioux, grew and became more widespread. Wagon trains, ranches, and stagecoach stations were attacked and often burned. Soldiers were sent to the Nebraska frontier. By the end of 1865, the main Indian troubles shifted further north and west. When the fort was no longer needed, it was closed on May 22, 1871, and the buildings were torn down. Today, it has been reconstructed so visitors can learn what the area was like in pioneer days.

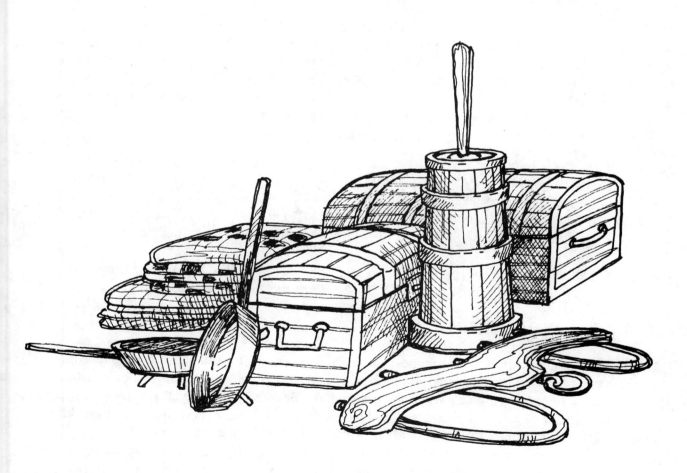

GA1473

Fort Kearny Activity

During the 1840s bison were plentiful on the Great Plains, including near Fort Kearny. In the early, plentiful years, emigrants shot and used bison wastefully, bringing the choice cuts of meat back to the wagons and leaving the bulk of the carcasses for the wolves. In 1847 Mormon pioneers spent so much time chasing bison that Brigham Young, their leader, called them together and in the words of Appleton Harmos, "said that thair should be no more game killed until such time as it should be needed for it was a Sin to waste life & flesh."

The animal commonly called the "buffalo" is really the American bison. The only true buffalo live in Asia and are usually called "water buffalo." Look at the pictures and notice the differences between these animals.

In those days there appeared to be an endless supply of bison. John Bidwell wrote in 1841, "I have seen the plain black with them for several days journey, as far as the eye could reach. They seemed to be coming northward continually from the distant plains to the Platte, to get water . . . ." After the slaughter of bison by the pioneers, it appeared the bison were all going to be killed. They have now been protected. There are about 100,000 bison in the United States today, and they are not in danger of extinction.

The bison were valuable as a source of fuel as well as meat. To cook their meals and warm themselves on the timberless plains, the pioneers depended heavily on the deposits of "buffalo chips"—dried dung—that were commonly found on the ground. Although they didn't want to handle chips at first, they soon learned chips would burn hotter than charcoal, last longer than wood, and strangely they would burn with no odor and practically no smoke. Bread, bacon, and coffee were the main parts of the pioneer diet. They added fresh meat, such as bison, when it was available. They often cut it into strips and dried it for future use.

Water Buffalo   **Bison**

Dry some meat and learn how this pioneer food tasted. Use beef if bison is not available. With the help of an adult, slice meat into long strips, about 1/4" (.6 cm) thick. Salt and pepper the meat. (Recipe books often give special recipes to make flavored jerky, which you may enjoy, but this would not be how the pioneers would have prepared it.) Place the strips on oven racks in single layers. Oven temperature should be 140° to 160° F (60° to 71° C) for the first 8 to 10 hours. After that, it may be lowered to 130° F (54° C) until dry. Place a cookie sheet under the racks to catch the drippings. Occasionally blot the jerky with paper towels as it dries, to remove beads of oil. Test jerky for dryness by cooling a piece. When cool, it should crack when bent but not break. There should be no moist spots. Jerky prepared in this way may be stored at room temperature for one to two months in a container with a loose-fitting lid. It may also be refrigerated or frozen in an airtight container.

GA1473

Windlass Hill and Ash Hollow

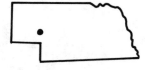

3¹/₂ miles (6 km) SE of Lewellen, NE
Garden County

Windlass Hill was the first steep grade encountered by the pioneers on the Oregon Trail. They came down this hill into Ash Hollow, a beautiful oasis and popular camping area with fresh spring water and plentiful grass for their livestock. The wheel ruts can still be seen on Windlass Hill, carved down 2' to 4' (.61 to 1.22 m) by the thousands of wagons that traveled the trail and from continued erosion.

There were several ways the pioneers got their wagons down this steep slope. Some tied ropes to the backs of their wagons and used "people power" to slow them. They would attach as many ropes as they had people and let the wagons go, with the people sliding their feet to provide as much braking power as possible. It was reported that one lady who was going down the hill this way was pulled right over a cactus! Others tied their oxen on the back of the wagons to act as brakes. Some locked the wheels, called rough-locking, to make them slide by chaining the front wheels to the back wheels or to the wagon box. The hill got its name from "windlass," a contraption for lowering wagons down a hill, but these are not mentioned in any emigrant journals that have been researched. If there ever was a windlass used here, it would have been after Oregon Trail emigration.

Although many emigrants wrote about the steepness of the grade, there were few accidents on the hill. One man wrote in 1849 that the descent was so breathtaking that no one spoke for two miles (3.2 km). That had to be an exaggeration. The hazardous part of the hill was less than a half mile (.8 km) long. The descent was described by one writer as breaking the monotony—also the legs of the horses, mules, and oxen, and the arms of the teamsters. If a wagon broke loose, and many did, it went tumbling down the hill in a shower of splinters.

Ash Hollow is a long plain stretching from Windlass Hill to the North Platte River. The pioneers were tired of the dry plains and looked forward to reaching Ash Hollow because of its springs and the shade of its cedar and ash trees. Emigrants could rest in this beautiful setting and repair wagons while their animals grazed the lush grasses. However, during the gold rush which started in 1849, the area became damaged due to many thoughtless people. Most of the trees were cut down, the springs became polluted, and cholera epidemics turned the area into a large cemetery.

Today, a visitor center is at Ash Hollow. There is a great variety of displays—geology, paleontology, history of native people, and the story of the pioneer journey west. Bones of prehistoric rhinoceros, mammoths, and small ancient mammals that once roamed the Great Plains have been found at Ash Hollow. A restored schoolhouse built of native stone is open to the public. During pioneer days trading posts were in the area too.

26

GA1473

Archaeological excavations in Ash Hollow indicate that early people used the area as much as 8000 years ago. A small rock shelter in the side of a bluff was used as a campsite by later Plains Indians for about 3000 years. One of the last Indian groups to have lived in the area was the Dismal River People, ancestors to the Plains Apache. Less than 100 years after the Dismal River People left the area, white fur traders were exploring the plains, followed a few years later by the pioneers.

The most famous grave at Ash Hollow and the one most often mentioned in emigrant journals is that of Rachel Pattison of Illinois. She was an 18-year-old bride of just two months when she died of cholera on June 19, 1849. Her husband, Nathan Pattison, recorded her death in his journal with this brief entry: "Rachel taken sick in the morning, died in the night." John McKieran, an emigrant of 1852, saw her grave and wrote, "May 16 . . . Poor thing! No doubt when she left home she anticipated that very much happiness which was to be hers but alas she now sleeps far very far from all that loved her. May such not be my fate."

Today, the Ash Hollow Cemetery can be visited. Although there were many graves in this area, Rachel Pattison's is the only identifiable grave from Oregon Trail days. With a death along the trail, there was little time to mourn. Graves were quickly dug and the people had to keep moving West. Nearly all the graves soon disappeared. Prairie wolves and coyotes quickly dug up all but the deepest burials. Wind, rain, and floods eroded the quickly-made headboards, and only a few of the best-marked graves kept their identity for very long.

Besides cholera, smallpox was another deadly disease that affected the emigrants. Theodore Potter wrote in 1852, "We passed through Ash Hollow . . . we counted over sixty graves by the roadside. As we approached the river valley we saw numerous wagons halted as far from the road as they could get, each flying a red flag to indicate the presence of smallpox."

The typical deaths among the pioneers were caused by accidents such as falling under the wagon wheels (often children), drownings, accidental shootings, and lightning strikes during thunderstorms with hail the size of apples. Very few pioneers were ever killed by Indians.

27

Windlass Hill and Ash Hollow Activity

Using other pieces of paper, create your own pioneer cemetery.

1. You will need white paper and a black or gray crayon without its paper wrapper.

2. Using the side of the crayon, make light rubbings on the bottom of several different tennis shoes. Don't rub the whole bottom, just the "toe" half, as shown, so it looks like an old gravestone. (Remember, most pioneers didn't have gravestones, but some graves were identified years later by relatives, and gravestones were added at that time.) Cut out your paper gravestones.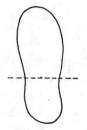

3. On each shoe-rubbing, write the name, life dates, and any other life events or epitaphs on this gravestone. Make them serious, to relate to real ways pioneers may have died. Use appropriate dates and typical names of the time.

4. After you have several gravestones, glue them onto a bigger paper and and draw the surrounding old cemetery. Name your cemetery.

GA147

Courthouse, Jail, and Chimney Rocks

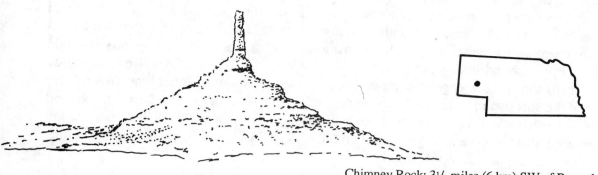

Chimney Rock

Chimney Rock: 3½ miles (6 km) SW of Bayard
Courthouse and Jail Rocks: 5 miles (8 km) south of Bridgeport
Morrill County, NE

These rock formations had been seen by the pioneers for miles and miles across the flat prairie and took some of the boredom out of the trip. Unlike traveling in a car today when you might see a rock and in just a few minutes pass it, these rocks were on the horizon for days and the pioneers had time to memorize their shapes.

Courthouse Rock and Jail Rock

In 1853 Thomas Flint wrote, "Court House Rock nearly opposite across the Platt. It is three stories high in appearance from the different stratifications. The jail is represented by a square bluff just east of the court house." Capt. Howard Stansbury who passed the rock with a group from the military in 1849 stated that the "...voyageurs, most of whom are originally from St. Louis, have given this name, from a fancied resemblance to a well known structure in their own city." Some say it looked like the statehouse in Jefferson City, Missouri, or the courthouse in Louisville, Kentucky, among others. The Jail name first appeared in the 1852 journal of John T. Kerns, "... There is a large rock on the south of court house which resembles a jail house."

On June 1, 1850, Orange Gaylord wrote, "went over & examined it [Courthouse] . . . found the names of thousands of immigrants cut on it . . . ." The rock was too soft to keep the carved names for more than a few years. There are only a few names left on it today. One emigrant wrote, however, that there was no room left on the entire rock for him to carve his own name. Walter G. Pigman wrote in 1850, "We spent an hour on the summit writing. Our heads became dizzy, we began to hunt the base and had a hard time to overtake our wagons and being nearly fifteen miles off we traveled hard but did not overtake them until they camped for the night. We had left camp without a gun, pistol or knife, which we ought to have had as the wolves and bears became unusually thick before we got in."

Chimney Rock

This is probably the most famous of all the great landmarks of the westward migration. Statistically, it is the most frequently noted and had the most written about it in pioneer journals. Some said it looked like a tall factory chimney or the chimney of a burned house. Warren A. Ferris described Chimney Rock in 1830 as a "limbless trunk of a gigantic tree." The Indians often called it "The Tepee" or "The Wigwam." In 1842 Elijah White said it reminded him of the Washington Monument. Joseph Hackney wrote in 1849 that Chimney Rock was "the most remarkable object that I ever saw and if situated in the states would be visited by persons from all parts of the world."

GA1473

A nearby spring made the Chimney Rock area a popular campsite. On June 7, 1832, Nathaniel Wyeth had less to say about the rock than he did about conditions near it: "my face so swelled from the musquitoes and ghnats that I can scarce see out of my eyes and aches like the tooth ache." Charles Preuss in 1842 wrote, "this afternoon we sighted at a distance the so-called Chimney Rock . . . nothing new otherwise . . . killed a cow today and the meat was cut up into very thin slices. They are hung around to dry and look like red curtins. . . ." Journals show Chimney Rock was often climbed, and there was great competition to carve one's name higher than anyone else had. Because of the soft nature of the rock, no pioneer names survive today. One lady cut foot and hand holes in the soft rock to help her climb high to find a carving spot. In 1849 James Mason Hutchings reported a name written 30 feet (9 m) up the rock and wrote, "one poor fellow had fallen and was killed" attempting to top the mark.

Sixty million years ago, deposits of soft sands and gravels were spread over this region from the Rocky Mountains. Later, volcanic action in these mountains added ash and other sediments to this area. Eventually, where there was harder, solidified rock on top, bluffs were left standing and the surrounding softer rock disappeared.

Courthouse Rock is divided into these separate rock sections:
Lower $1/4$: Brule clay
Middle $1/2$: Coarse sand and soft sandstone
Top $1/4$: Gray sands, volcanic ash, and capped with solidified rock

Jail Rock   **Courthouse Rock**

Chimney Rock today is composed entirely of Brule clay with some layers of volcanic ash. The top layer, which is now eroded away, was probably the harder Arickaree sandstone with a concentration of limestone layers.

Most pioneer journal writers who didn't have a knowledge of geology came to the conclusion that Chimney Rock was composed of a very perishable material which was rapidly eroding. Part of the miracle of Chimney Rock was that no one could explain how this soft rock happened to be standing so far up in the air. P.F. Castleman wrote in 1849, "It is wasting away very fast and I dare say in a few years this old and weather beaten rock will entirely waste away." In 1855 William Chandless wrote, "The rain, that has caused the remarkable shape, is now rapidly lessening and destroying the object."

The rock was stronger than the pioneers had predicted. Today, Chimney Rock stands 375 feet (114 m). A lightning bolt knocked 17 feet (5.2 m) off it in 1972. Another large piece reportedly fell off in April 1927. It has been said that the emigrants and also the U.S. Army used the rock for shooting practice before that. From 1885 until today there has been an erosion of only 17 feet, (5.2 m) by actual scientific measure.

GA147

Courthouse, Jail, and Chimney Rocks Activity

Use one of these recipes (or another favorite clay recipe) and sculpt the shape of either Chimney, Courthouse, or Jail Rock. Place your sculpture on heavy cardboard or wood and label it with the name of the rock.

Possible recipes:

1. **Sand Sculpting:** Mix two parts sand, one part water, and one part cornstarch. Heat and stir the mixture until it's thick. Let the mixture cool. Then use your hands to mold it into the rock. Let your creation dry and harden.

2. **Modeling Clay:** Add food coloring (to make a light yellow-brown) to 1¼ cups (300 ml) cold water. Mix well with 1 cup (240 ml) cornstarch and 2 cups (480 ml) baking soda in a saucepan. Cook over medium heat about 3 to 4 minutes, stirring constantly until the mixture thickens to the consistency of mashed potatoes. Cover with a damp cloth to cool. Knead until smooth. Sculpt your rock. Let it dry overnight. It can be painted if you wish. Store unused clay in an airtight container.

To show the layers of Courthouse Rock, try making a geology sandwich. Here is one way.
    Bottom layer: one slice of white bread for Brule clay
    Middle layer: chunky peanut butter and jelly for coarse sand and soft sandstone
    Top layer: one slice of "grainy" brown bread for harder gray sands and volcanic ash

Another way to make a geology sandwich is shown below.

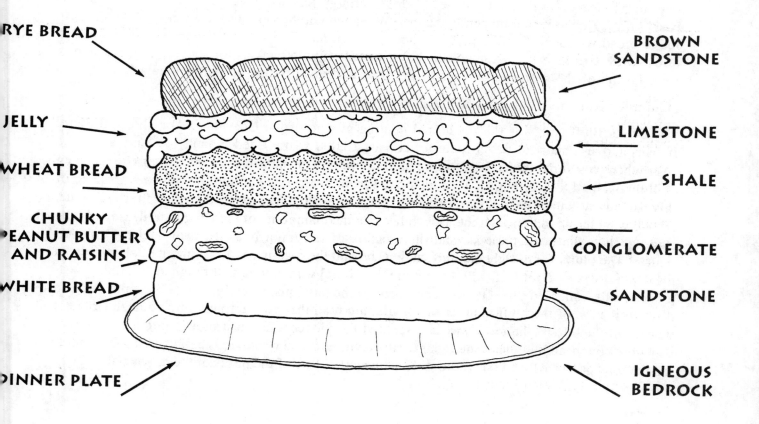

RYE BREAD — BROWN SANDSTONE
JELLY — LIMESTONE
WHEAT BREAD — SHALE
CHUNKY PEANUT BUTTER AND RAISINS — CONGLOMERATE
WHITE BREAD — SANDSTONE
DINNER PLATE — IGNEOUS BEDROCK

GA1473

Scotts Bluff National Monument

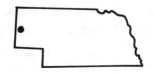

3 miles (5 km) west of Gering, NE
5 miles (8 km) SW of Scottsbluff, NE
Scotts Bluff County

Scotts Bluff is an 800-foot (243.8-m) mass of clay and sandstone that formed millions of years ago when rivers deposited sand and gravel here. It is part of the same eroding range of hills as Courthouse Rock and Chimney Rock. Scotts Bluff is the largest. This unusual rock formation was described by A.J. McCall on June 14, 1849: "They are . . . cliffs of . . . clay, bearing resemblance to towers, castles, churches, and fortified cities . . . ." During the early days of the trail, emigrants traveled over Robidoux Pass. In 1851, Mitchell Pass was cut through by the Army, taking off eight difficult miles (12.8 km). Today, Nebraska Highway 92 runs right through the pass, but in pioneer days the wagons had to leave the river and had a hard pull over the difficult ridge at Mitchell Pass. William H. Jackson wrote in 1866: "We drove up to & into the pass . . . . We had one of the steepest and worst gulches to drive through that we have yet had. Got through [the pass] safely. Had quite a time getting supper. When we got the keg out for water to make the coffee & bread we found that the precious liquid was minus. The nearest water was some 3 miles away. [N. Platte River] . . . some of the boys started off with buckets for some . . . . Our camp is right in one of the narrowest places of the pass & the walls rise up perpendicularly on either hand."

The Scotts Bluff area was the traditional hunting ground of the Cheyenne, Arapaho, and Sioux Indians and an important travel route for at least 10,000 years. It led Indians to places along the river where wandering bison herds stopped to drink. Indians named the spot Me-a-pa-te meaning "hill that is hard to go around." Visitors today can see deep ruts cut into the soft rock roadbed of this narrow mountain pass. Years of heavy wagon traffic cut through the rock. In 1852 alone, 50,000 wagons moved through the pass. It became the main route of the Oregon trail, the military, stagecoaches, the Pony Express, and the location of telegraph lines. In 1856 Helen Carpenter wrote: "The bluffs are of light colored sandy clay—and the road is cut down into it . . . in places, to the depth of six or eight feet, with little more than [one] wagon to pass through . . . ." Today, visitors can still walk along the Oregon Trail through the pass, just as emigrants did. People can also drive to the top of the bluff along a steep, winding road that goes through three tunnels, to get a wonderful view from the top. They can see that the pioneers had just passed through the plains and were now heading toward the mountains. David E. Pease wrote on June 2, 1849: "This morning the road passed over the ridge from which we saw some of the peaks of the mountains . . . ."

GA1473

Emigrants were interested in the story of how Scotts Bluff was named, and many wrote about it in their diaries. There are many variations to the story but the following is one of the common versions: In 1828 Miram Scott, a fur trader, became sick as he and his two companions were traveling down the North Platte River. About sixty miles (97 km) from the bluff where the three were to meet with other trappers, Scott became too sick to travel. The other men were sure he was near death and abandoned him. Somehow Scott made his way alone to the meeting location, only to find that the men had left and there was no help for him. He crawled to a spring at the base of the bluff and died. Later, his skeleton was found at the bluff that became named for him. Somehow he had traveled about sixty miles (97 km) before dying.

William Henry Jackson

William Henry Jackson was a well-known frontier artist and photographer. A large collection of his works are displayed at the Scotts Bluff National Monument visitor center. His work has helped later generations know what natural and pioneer sites looked like during frontier days.

He learned art at an early age since his mother was an artist and his father was a photographer. In the Infantry during the Civil War he spent most of his time sketching military maps, forts, and portraits of soldiers. After the war, he returned to Vermont, thinking he would work at a gallery and get married. However, according to Jackson, "In April, 1866, I . . . was engaged to be married in June. The engagement was broken, and I . . . decided to get away as quickly and as far as I could." He headed for the Missouri River and took a job as a bullwhacker which he described as yoking half-wild cattle and forcing them to pull wagons. He traveled through Nebraska, Wyoming, and into Utah. These travels left a lasting impression on Jackson, and for the next seventy years he sketched, wrote about, and photographed the West.

His frontier photographs were so good that he was hired as a member of Dr. Ferdinand Haydon's U.S. Geological Survey expeditions exploring the Rocky Mountain region. He gained fame as the "Pioneer Photographer." His photographs helped convince the 1871-72 Congress to designate Yellowstone as our country's first national park. He also photographed the Colorado Rocky Mountains, the Grand Teton Mountains, and ancient Indian ruins in the Southwest. After the Hayden expeditions, he developed a photography career that took him all over the United States and the world. At age 81, his business went broke and he had no way to make a living. Jackson remembered the sketches and writings of his early years in the West, which he had ignored for years. He painted watercolor scenes based on his frontier travels. His accurate memory helped him produce hundreds of paintings showing life and events of the American West. Jackson died in 1942 at age 99.

GA1473

Scotts Bluff National Monument Activity

Now it's your turn to become a frontier artist.

- You will need three pieces of white drawing paper and either crayons, colored pencils, or paints.
- Color picture frames around all three pieces of paper.
- On scratch paper, sketch a pioneer scene from western Nebraska, such as Courthouse and Jail Rocks, Chimney Rock, or Scotts Bluff.
- On the first paper, color your western Nebraska picture inside the frame. Draw it in a *realistic* style like William H. Jackson might have drawn.
- On the second paper, again color the same western Nebraska picture inside the frame but this time draw it in a *modern art* style.
- On the third paper, again color the same western Nebraska picture inside the frame but this time draw it in an *impressionistic* style.
  Note: You may have to do some research to learn the difference between realism, modern, and impressionistic styles.
- Display your three pictures together. Label them with the name of the scene, such as Scotts Bluff and also label them with the styles of art that you have used–realism, modern art, and impressionism.

Fort Laramie National Historic Site
1834-1890

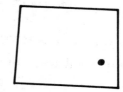

3 miles (5 km) SW of Fort Laramie, WY
Goshen County

Over the years, as the West developed, Fort Laramie changed its role from an Indian trading post to emigrant resting place to military center. Trappers, traders, missionaries, emigrants, Pony Express riders, and miners stopped here.

In 1834 fur trader William Sublette decided to have a trading post built at this location beside the Laramie River. A fort would make it easier to bring supplies west and take beaver furs and bison robes back east. Two years later the American Fur Company bought the fort, and in 1841 it built a new whitewashed adobe fort to replace the old one that was rotting. By the 1880s, Fort Laramie looked somewhat like a frontier town, but for many early years it was a plain collection of military buildings in a treeless setting. Most of the people living at the fort were males, although there were a few officers' wives and some laundresses.

Fort Laramie became a center for Indian trade, with more than 10,000 bison robes purchased each year. Traders generally paid $1.00 per robe in the form of gunpowder, hatchets, tobacco, coffee, sugar, blankets, beads, and liquor. Robes were then sold for a profit in St. Louis for $4.00 each. A large Indian village of tipis was always around the fort.

As the fur trade gradually ended, traders found that money could be made by selling supplies to emigrants. Fort Laramie stood along the main trail to Oregon and California. It was located one-third of the way between Missouri and the end of the trail so it provided a much anticipated break before the long, dry stretches of trail ahead. Emigrants stopped to repair wagons, purchase supplies, or trade tired stock for fresh oxen and horses. Fort Laramie was one of the few dependable post offices along the trail with monthly mail service. Emigrants remembered it as a good place to learn what was happening back in "the States" and to hear the rumors from Oregon.

In 1849 the Army purchased Fort Laramie for $4000 to protect the Oregon Trail from Indian attacks. In the early days of the fort, Indians and pioneers got along fairly peacefully, but troubles grew as the Indians' way of life became threatened. The fort also served as a meeting place to make treaty arrangements with the Indians of the region.

Fort Laramie was not a pleasant place. The food was awful and the sanitary conditions were bad. The discipline was so strict that even the smallest mistake could land a man in the bare, unheated guardhouse jail. Things were so bad that it was no wonder that the five-year enlistments in the Army seemed to never end. Between 1865 and 1890, 33 percent of the men deserted, many leaving for the gold fields in California.

GA1473

36

By 1890, Fort Laramie was no longer needed and was ordered closed. The next year, the land was opened to homesteaders. In 1938, President Franklin Roosevelt declared Fort Laramie a national monument, and the difficult process began to restore the historic structures. Today, tourists can visit the fort and see living history presentations of life at the fort.

The emigration of the pioneers along the Oregon Trail had its negative side. Children's geography books of these years described the region the pioneers crossed as the "Great American Desert" but the U.S. Government had designated it as Indian land. The pioneer wagon trains were clearly trespassing. The Indian way of life was being destroyed. There was a lack of understanding on both sides. Some Indians felt the settlers had "powerful medicine," with their wagons, utensils, religion, trinkets, and weapons. To some pioneers, the Indians appeared to be "savages" with no right to the land. The Indians could not understand why treaties with the settlers were only honored for a short time. The Indians were not immune from the European diseases brought by the settlers and many died. Bison were being shot and forced from their traditional migration routes, and thousands of stock brought by the emigrants were destroying the grasslands.

Conflicts began as Indians sometimes stopped wagon trains and demanded "tolls" in the form of tobacco, coffee, sugar, or other goods. If the emigrants cooperated, there was usually no further trouble. Pioneer journals describe many, many examples of times when the Indians were a great help to them, and they often enjoyed trading with each other. Lydia Allen Rudd wrote on August 14, 1852, "Bought a salmon fish of an indian today weighing seven or eight pounds. Gave him an old shirt and some bread and a sewing needle." The emigrants had a great fear of the Indians but rarely were there attacks. These attacks usually took the form of raids on livestock which left the wagons unharmed. Often the fear of attack killed and injured pioneers because loaded rifles in the wagons accidentally discharged. Of the 350,000 pioneers to travel West, only about 350 were ever killed by the Indians. (Approximately 30,000 people died on the trail between 1843 and 1859, which averages about one grave for every 100 yards [91 m] of the trail from the Missouri River to the Willamette River.) Attacks increased as the Indians realized their homelands were disappearing forever. Emigrants demanded to be protected so Congress gave Fort Laramie a new role as a military post to guard the trail.

The following story is one example of the role the military played. In August of 1854, a young officer from Fort Laramie made a mistake that started much of the hostility toward the pioneers. A Mormon's lame cow wandered away from the wagon train and ended up in a Sioux village south of the fort. The Mormons were afraid to ask to have the cow back so they reported their loss to the Army. Lt. John L. Grattan took twenty-nine soldiers with him to retrieve the cow, which by this time had been killed. Grattan unwisely forced a fight that resulted in the death of Grattan, all of his men, and an Indian chief. Many years of hostilities between the Indians and pioneers followed this incident.

GA1473

Fort Laramie National Historic Site Activity

Imagine that you are an adult pioneer on the Oregon Trail. The Indians have stopped your wagon train and do not want you to continue your journey. The Indians are concerned that their way of life is being destroyed because of the large number of emigrants. Write the list of arguments you use to convince the Indians to let you pass and continue your journey to Oregon.

Central Wyoming

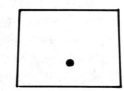

Central Wyoming
Between Guernsey and Devil's Gate
Platte and Natrona Counties

Deep Rut Hill and Register Cliff
South of Guernsey, WY, Platte County
To avoid eating dust from the wagons ahead, out on the plains the wagons did not follow in a single-file line. However, at Deep Rut Hill, the wagons were forced into one route between a hill and the river. The route was over soft sandstone so the ruts cut down as deep as five feet (1.5 m) in some places! Nearby is Register Cliff, a mile-long cliff where many emigrants carved their names in the rock. "We came along the base of a large bluff that was covered up as far as a person could reach with names and dates of those that have passed this way," wrote Delila B. Saunders on July 9, 1866.

Fort Caspar (1858-1867)
West side of Casper, WY, Natrona County
Fort Caspar was a military post named for Lt. Caspar Collins. It was established at the Oregon Trail crossing of the North Platte River to guard the Platte Bridge. Today, the fort has been reconstructed to its original appearance.

High winds and high water made this river crossing very dangerous. In 1847, before any bridges were built, Brigham Young, the leader of the Mormons, decided money could be made by building a ferry and charging emigrants a fee to raft their wagons across the river. Over the years, more ferries came and eventually bridges were built. These were expensive for the emigrants but made the river crossing much safer.

Independence Rock
50 miles (80.5 km) SW of Casper, WY, Natrona County
Independence Rock, a large oval-shaped granite outcropping, was an important Oregon Trail landmark because of its large size. It is 1950 feet (594.4 m) long, 850 feet (259 m) wide, and at its highest point it is 193 feet (58.8 m) tall. In 1837 Alfred Jacob Miller wrote that from ten miles (16.1 km) away "we were struck with its resemblance to a huge tortoise sprawling in the desert." Emigrants knew it was important to arrive at Independence Rock by July 4th to improve their chances of getting to Oregon before the snow fell.

Devil's Gate

7 miles (11.27 km) SW of Independence Rock, Natrona County

Devil's Gate is a narrow cut where the Sweetwater River breaks through the Rattlesnake Mountains. It was a gloomy, violent place when the water was high so it seemed appropriate to be called Devil's Gate. Capt. Howard Stansbury wrote in 1853: "A kanyon of steep rocks, 400 feet high (where) the river runs through the chasm." The Oregon Trail passed a half mile (.8 km) south of here so emigrants often hiked over to see the gorge. Martha Missouri Moore wrote on July 23, 1860: "Visited the Devil's Gate the most noted curiosity along this road. This is indeed wonderful to look at . . . ."

Along this stretch of trail in 1856, a Mormon handcart company was delayed on the trail and became trapped by snow. They waited desperately, in what became known as Martin's Cove, for a relief crew from Utah. They eventually were rescued but not before 145 people had died.

In 1840, Father Pierre-Jean De Smet, a Catholic missionary, wrote: "Independence Rock is the great register of the desert, the names of all the travelers who have passed by are there to read, written in coarse character; mine figures among them."

Emigrants often left their names on large rocks along the trail such as Independence Rock, Register Cliff, and Devil's Gate, and on bleached bones found on the ground. These were places to look for messages from friends who had traveled on ahead or to leave word for those who were coming from behind. Some people wrote their names on the rocks just to record that they had been there.

It is estimated that 50,000 names were carved, chipped, or painted on Independence Rock during the mid-19th century. To chip into the rocks, they used chisels or similar tools. Some painted the letters on with mixtures such as pine tar and hog fat that was used to grease wagon axles. Since some were illiterate and couldn't write, they often asked someone else to write for them. Some Mormons who were experienced stonecutters set up "business" at Independence Rock and charged from $1 to $5 for each name carved on the rock.

Today, hundreds of names are still visible on Independence Rock. Some names have been "rubbed off" by lichens (small mosslike plants), known as "Mother Nature's erasers." Others have been weathered off. To protect the carvings from recent vandals who have added their own names on top of the pioneer names, much of the rock's face has been fenced.

Independence Rock

Devil's Gate

GA1473

Central Wyoming Activity

When emigrants took the time to leave their names behind on rocks or bones, they usually wrote in beautiful lettering, the style that was taught in schools of those days. Using the "old-fashioned" alphabet below, write a pioneer trail message on the bison skull. On the cliff, write your name and a year (that was during emigrant times).

41

South Pass

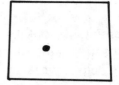

Summit of the Continental Divide
45 miles (72 km) SW of Lander, WY
Fremont County

When the emigrants reached the top of South Pass they had traveled about halfway from Missouri to Oregon. Agnes Stewart wrote in 1853: "I am weary of this journey. I long for the quiet of home where I can be at peace once more." There were many difficult miles ahead, but they had now reached the unofficial boundary of the Oregon Territory. "Here Hail Oregon," wrote Joel Palmer in 1845 as his wagon reached the summit (7550 feet [2301 m]). At this point they crossed the Continental Divide, the highest point in the United States. This meant that if water was poured on the ground on one side of South Pass, it would eventually flow to the Atlantic Ocean. Water poured on the other side would eventually reach the Pacific Ocean.

The pioneers imagined that crossing the Rocky Mountains would be very difficult. They pictured it as a steep, narrow trail where they would have to travel single file. To their surprise, it was a nearly flat plain stretching for miles in all directions. The earth appeared to meet the sky. They couldn't imagine it was the top of the North American continent because it looked no different than the hundreds of dry, treeless miles of sagebrush that they had been crossing. They had been climbing gradually but it appeared to be so flat that usually the emigrants couldn't tell when they passed from one side to the other. Rev. Samuel Parker wrote on August 10, 1835: "The passage through these mountains is in a valley so gradual in the ascent and descent that I should not have known that we were passing them had it not been that as we advanced the atmosphere gradually became cooler . . . ." On June 18, 1849, James A. Pritchard wrote: "About 4 p.m. we stood upon the Summit level of the Rocky Mountains . . . 'the Backbone of the North American Continent'–And from which the waters flow into the Atlantic and Pacific Ocean . . . The Plateau of the South Pass is from 15 to 20 miles wide . . . ."

The emigrants rarely stopped at South Pass. They knew fresh water was only a few miles away at Pacific Springs. Charles Stanton wrote on July 19, 1846: ". . . came to a fine spring, with the grass looking green about it. The managers of our company finding it rather boggy, thought the cattle would get mired should they attempt to feed upon the rich herbage, and concluded to go on . . . the first water that flowed westward."

If this fairly easy route for crossing the Rocky Mountains had not been found, the Oregon Country might not have become part of the United States or at least it would have been much delayed. It would have been too difficult to get wagons and families over the mountains. Indians had used the route for many years. The first white man to find the pass was probably Robert Stuart who was returning with other explorers from the Columbia River, heading east. He wrote on October 22, 1812: "We set out at day light, and ascended about 3 miles, when we found a spring of excellent water, and breakfasted; 5 more brought us to the top of the mountain . . . ." Capt. Bonneville took the first wagon over South Pass in 1832. Between 1841 and 1866, over 350,000 people may have crossed the Rockies here. Gold was discovered in 1867. South Pass City, 12 miles (19.3 km) northeast of the pass, was a boomtown for a few years. Here the Wyoming Territorial Legislature met on December 10, 1869, and became the first legislature in U.S. history to grant equal voting rights to women.

Captain Benjamin Bonneville

Fort Bridger
1843-1890

At Fort Bridger State Park
Fort Bridger, WY
Uinta County

The Fort Bridger trading post was built on Black's Fork of the Green River in 1843 by Jim Bridger and his partner, Louis Vasquez. Bridger went West from St. Louis in 1822 as a member of the Ashley-Henry Fur Company and soon was known as a trapper, trader, and guide during the height of the fur-trapping years. As the supply of beaver ran out and the number of pioneers passing through the areas steadily increased, Bridger built his trading post mainly for the pioneer trade.

Fort Bridger was an important stop along the Oregon Trail. This was a place where pioneers could buy supplies, get blacksmith work done, and where worn out oxen, mules, and horses could be exchanged for fresh animals. The fort was often a disappointment to the emigrants. It was built out of wood which was packed over with adobe mud. Inside the walls were several log buildings and a horse corral. The most frequent complaint was that often the fort was unoccupied. Emigrants would often arrive needing help, but all the workers would be away. (Some pioneers took the Sublette Cut-Off which opened in 1844 and bypassed Fort Bridger. It saved about 46 miles [74 km], but it included 50 waterless miles [81 km].)

An interesting description of the early days of the fort was provided by Jim Bridger. Although he could neither read nor write, he got someone in 1843 to write a letter announcing, "I have established a small fort, with a blacksmith shop and supply of iron, in the road of the emigrants on Black Fork of Green River, which promises fairly. In coming out here they are in need of all kinds of supplies, horses, provisions, smithwork, etc. They bring ready cash from the states, and should I receive the goods ordered, will have considerable business in that way with them, and establish trade with the Indians in the neighborhood who have a good number of beaver among them."

The Mormons, heading to Salt Lake City in Utah, hoping to freely practice their religion, stopped at Fort Bridger to rest and buy supplies. In 1855 they bought the fort and used it for two years. There were arguments between the new Mormon state of Utah and the U.S. government. As a result, President James Buchanan sent U.S. troops to the area in 1857. As the troops approached, the Mormons burned the fort and fled to Utah.

GA1473

The fort was rebuilt and became a U.S. Army post. During 1860-61 the fort served as a station on the Pony Express route. It was also on the overland stagecoach routes. As hostilities between Indians and pioneers lessened in the West, the fort declined in importance. The last soldiers left on November 6, 1890. The reconstructed fort is now open for visitors.

When visiting the fort, one can see the grave of Thornburgh, a dog. This heroic dog was named for Major T.T. Thornburgh who was killed in an Indian attack. When the army arrived to bury the dead, they found this puppy and named it after the major. The dog never liked "sneaks" and over the years caught thieves, warned of potential Indian attacks, and rescued a boy from drowning. Eventually the dog ended up at Fort Bridger and was treated royally. In 1888 he was killed by a kick from a mule. His gravestone says, "Man never had a better, truer, braver friend. Sleep on, old fellow, we'll meet across the range."

Jim Bridger

GA1473

Fort Bridger Activity

Pretend that you are a pioneer family heading west to Oregon. When you started the journey at Independence, Missouri, you loaded your wagon with $400 worth of goods. (See the chart on page 12.) As you have traveled along, some of your things have been lost, broken, some even floated away during river crossings, and some were traded to the Indians. You have hot deserts to cross and then will be coming to the Blue Mountains and to the Cascade Range. The mountains are very steep and will be hard to cross. Your oxen will be tired and will not be able to pull a heavy load. At that time it will be necessary for you to throw out some of your belongings. Weight will be the biggest consideration. Since you just have these supplies listed by price on the chart and not by weight, choose another $150.00 worth of items that you must leave behind. Remember that you are doing this to help the oxen, so consider the weight. (So many things were thrown out along the Oregon Trail that people joked that you would have had to have been blind not to be able to follow the route because you'd just follow all the supplies that were left behind! Captain Howard Stansbury wrote in 1852, "The road is strewn with articles thrown away . . . I recognize the trunks of some of the passengers who had accompanied me from St. Louis to Kansas . . . .")

After you have made your list, write a paragraph explaining why you chose (and did not choose) the items you did. You will have to look at your work from the Independence Square page in order to know what your choices are.

Fort Hall
1834-1856

Upper level of Ross Park
Pocatello, Idaho
Bannock County

Fort Hall was built in 1834 as a fur-trading post by Nathaniel Wyeth, an American from Boston. There were plentiful game and many fur-bearing animals in the area which brought hunters and trappers. Rufus B. Sage wrote on November 4, 1842, "Fort Hall is located on the left bank of the Snake River . . . for the purpose of furnishing trappers with their needful supplies in exchange for beaver and other peltries, and to command the trade with the Snakes [Snake Indians]." Many kinds of animals were trapped for their furs–beaver, mink, sea otter, marten, and others. The thick, soft fur of the beaver was especially valued because it could be made into top hats, the fashion of the day for men. These were also called stovetop hats. The hats were made from the hair, not the pelts, of the beaver. Beaver hair has tiny barbs on it, and when the hair is removed from the pelt and compressed, it makes a very strong and attractive felt cloth. Beaver pelts became worth so much money that they were called "brown gold." Furs were valuable and could be used for trading. Since money was of little use in the wilderness, prices were often set in beaver pelts.

There were three main types of traders who brought pelts to the forts. Some men worked for companies, such as the Hudson's Bay Company, run by the British. Some were free trappers, such as the American mountain men who sold to the person who paid them the most. Some of these men had their families with them in the wilderness. Indians were also trappers, either for their own use or to trade for goods at the forts' trading posts. Items that were usually available at these forts included blankets, cloth, beads, fish hooks, needles, thread, mirrors, knives, food, and similar items. John Boardman wrote on August 11, 1843, ". . . it is inferior to Fort Laramie . . . there was neither meat, flour nor rice to be had. Nothing but sugar and coffee at 50 cents per pint."

At this time in the West, the British and the Americans were each trying to control as much land as possible so they could have the most trapping lands. The Hudson's Bay Company built a fort of its own nearby, called Fort Boise. Its purpose was simply to drive Fort Hall out of business. Wyeth was never able to make a decent profit, so in 1837 he sold the fort to the British at a loss of about $30,000.

The main fur trade came to an end by the early 1840s when furs had become more and more scarce from overtrapping. Also, at this time, the fashion which had been in demand for hundreds of years changed. Silk became popular, replacing beaver for men's hats, so the price of pelts fell. After 1849, Fort Hall was used mostly by the pioneers heading West. It was one of the most important stops on the Oregon Trail. Eventually, the fort started losing money. There were also increasing hostilities with the Indians as more and more emigrants came to the Indian lands, so the British eventually abandoned the fort in 1856.

Today, a replica of Fort Hall can be visited in Pocatello. The original site of the fort was on the east bank of the Snake River between the mouths of the Portneuf and Bannock Rivers. The river area had been used for years as a favorite food-gathering and camping place for the Shoshone-Bannock Indians and is now used only by the tribe.

The search for fur-bearing animals was responsible for much of the early exploration of the West. Mountain men and early emigrants found trapping to be an important source of money. It was hard and dangerous work because most of it was done in the winter when the animal pelts were the thickest. This trapping was so successful that the survival of some species became threatened. Other species such as wolves, cougars, bobcats, and coyotes preyed on the growing herds of the settlers and were trapped as predators.

Bounties were first established by the Oregon Territorial Government in 1843 to control these losses. Eventually, laws were passed to protect the furbearers. The first was passed by the Oregon Legislature in 1893 to provide a closed season on beaver in two counties.

The Federal Endangered Species Act of 1969 has helped control the legalized sale of fur, especially the pelts of rare animals. However, some animals are still facing extinction due to the actions of people.

Fort Hall Activity

Draw and name animals that are endangered today because of being so valued by people that they are overhunted. Tell why each animal is being hunted.

Animal Picture	Name of Animal	Use of Animal
	Elephant	Ivory tusks for jewelry

49

GA1473

Three Island Crossing

2 miles (3 km) SW of Glenns Ferry, Idaho
Elmore County

Three Island Crossing was where the pioneers tried to cross to the north side of the Snake River. The river was wider here, and there were three islands connected by natural sandbars. They often didn't use the third island but it depended on the water level. The crossing was always dangerous because the water was so clear that it appeared to be very shallow but was usually 6 to 8 feet (1.82 to 2.44 m) deep. Detailed instructions were given in guidebooks to avoid accidents, but drownings of people and animals still occurred and wagons often tipped over. Many times two wagons would be joined side by side to make the crossing easier. Pioneers used this crossing until 1869 when a ferry was put in about two miles (3 km) upstream.

On September 24, 1844, Rev. Edward Parrish wrote: "We crossed the river safely after noon today and camped on a fine bed of grass within sight of the ford. The river is rapid and the water . . . low. The bottom is gravel of the prettiest kind and the water is clear." Pioneer Peter H. Burnett wrote on September 10, 1843: "On the 10th of September we crossed the Snake River by fording without difficulty, and in crossing, we killed a salmon weighing 23 pounds, one of our wagons running over it as it lay on the bottom of the pebbly stream."

The emigrants tried to cross to the north side of the Snake River at Three Island Crossing because this would give them a better route to Fort Boise. The pioneers on the south side found a desert of deep sand, extreme heat, and dry vegetation. Samuel James wrote on July 24, 1850: "The most desolate country in the whole world. The region of the shadow of death." Those on the south side rejoined the main Oregon Trail just west of Fort Boise in what is Eastern Oregon today.

Overton Johnson and William H. Winter were in the Applegate group in 1843 and wrote: "We came to the crossing . . . having attempted the crossing and finding it too deep, were obliged to continue down to the South. This is, perhaps, the most rugged, desert and dreary country, between the Western borders of the United States and the shores of the Pacific. It is nothing less than a wild, rocky barren wilderness, of wrecked and ruined Nature, a vast field of volcanic desolation."

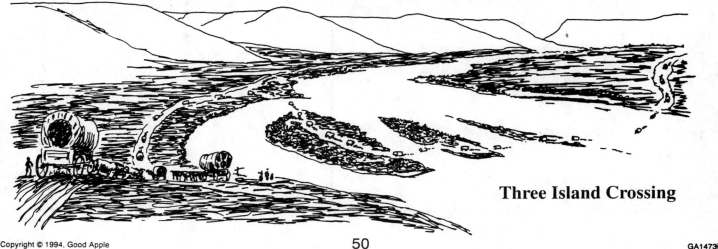

Three Island Crossing

GA1473

In this area, emigrant contacts with Indians were usually friendly ones. The Shoshone and Bannock tribes would often trade food to pioneers for old clothing or other things they needed. Indians would also help the emigrants in river crossings and finding trails. In 1843, Lt. John Charles Fremont, on a federal exploring expedition, camped among the Indians. He described their lodges as "semi-circular huts made of willow, thatched over with straw, and open to the sunny south." However, the Three Island Crossing area sometimes was a dangerous area for conflict and misunderstanding between the pioneers and Indians. P.V. Crawford wrote on August 1, 1851, the third day of their river crossing: "This day we completed crossing our fifteen wagons before night. Last night we had three horses stolen, and three more shot in the shoulders with arrows. Grass is good here, but Indians are very bad."

Three Island Crossing is now an Idaho State Park with a visitor center and displays of bison and longhorn cattle. Wagon ruts can be seen coming down the hills on the south bank.

51

Three Island Crossing Activity

Three Island Crossing was such a dangerous river ford that emigrants often wrote about it in their journals. Newspaper reporters weren't along on the journey, so much that is known about the Oregon Trail is from journals and letters that were written at the time.

Imagine that you were a newspaper reporter at Three Island Crossing. Write newspaper-style accounts of trail life near Three Island Crossing, such as preparing for the crossing, the river crossing itself, contact with the Indians, traveling or camping on the north side of the Snake River, and traveling on the dry south side of the Snake River.

Do *each type* of newspaper writing using the Three Island Crossing topic.

1. **News Story**
   A news story should contain information based on proven facts and should not contain personal opinions. Important facts are placed at the beginning of the story and things not so important go further down in the story. In that way, if the story is too long and the editor has to shorten it, the important things won't be cut out. The five W's go at the beginning of the story: who, what, where, when, why (and sometimes how). The purpose is not to entertain but to inform and should be done briefly, concisely, accurately, and completely.

   Include a headline also. A headline tells the main idea of the story. It has to introduce news in a way that will make the reader want to know more. It can't take up much space. It does not have to be a complete sentence.

2. **Feature Story**
   Feature stories give background information and people's reactions. They have more to do with emotions and feelings than news stories. They tell of the human story behind the news so they are also called human interest stories. Here are several different types of feature stories that you may wish to choose from: seasons, hobbies or amusement, travel, beauty, children, animals, background material for some event, holidays, reminiscence (remember when . . .). These stories also contain the five W's. They are written in a more casual, friendly, informal style. Put a headline on this story.

3. **Editorial**
   Editorials present opinions as well as give information. This is the place where writers tell what they think. This writing tries to persuade the reader to agree with an opinion. Editorials also contain the five W's and a headline.

4. **Advertisement**
   This could be written two ways:
   a. Pretend there was a small store at Three Island Crossing. Write an advertisement for what it might sell to the emigrants.
   b. Write a classified ad for something you, as a pioneer, would like to buy or sell.

5. **Comic or Cartoon**
   Draw a single-frame or multi-frame cartoon that shows the humor of the situation the emigrants faced at Three Island Crossing. This could also be done as an editorial (political) cartoon.

Fort Boise
1834-1854

Original fort: 4.7 miles (8 km) NW of Parma, Idaho
Replica of fort: In the town of Parma, Canyon County

The Hudson's Bay Company began building this fort at the junction of the Boise and Snake Rivers in 1834. It was completed in 1835 and was built to compete in the fur trade with Fort Hall that belonged to the Americans. Tom McKay, the stepson of John McLaughin, was the head of the fort. The fort did so well that it was replaced by an adobe building on the east bank of the Snake River eight miles (13 km) north of the Boise River. Outside the fort were horse corrals, and inside were housing, a blacksmith shop, and stores. As the fur trade declined after 1840, the fort began to depend on business from the Oregon Trail emigrants. Emigrants were able to purchase some needed supplies and get help in ferrying across the Snake River.

An 1845 report said, "Two acres of land under cultivation . . . 1991 sheep, 73 pigs, 17 horses, and 27 meat cattle." There were 300 miles (483 km) of desert between Fort Hall and Fort Boise so this was a welcome oasis.

Fort Boise was important in the progress of wheeled vehicles across the West. Dr. Marcus Whitman, a missionary, brought his two-wheeled cart to Fort Boise on August 19, 1836. The cart was the half of his wagon that remained after the front axle broke east of Fort Hall. This was the farthest a wheeled wagon had gone. (By 1840, three complete wagons got to Fort Boise and on across the Snake River to Walla Walla.)

The day after Narcissa Whitman, the wife of Marcus, arrived at the fort, she did laundry for the third time in her long journey from Independence. Her journal for August 22nd says, "Left the Fort yesterday. Came a short distance to the crossing of the Snake river, crossed and encamped for the night . . . . As for the wagon, it is left at the fort, and I have nothing to say about crossing it at this time. Five of our cattle were left there also, to be exchanged for others at Walla Walla. Perhaps you will wonder why we have left the wagon, having taken it so nearly through. Our animals are failing, and the route in crossing the Blue Mountains is said to be impassable for it."

Floods every few years, especially in 1853, plus the decline in the fur trade, were hardships on the fort. In 1846 the boundary dispute with England was settled, and Fort Boise was then under the laws of the United States. There was Indian trouble in 1854 and soon the fort was abandoned completely.

Over the years, the Snake River has wandered in its path and today the site of the fort is under the river. Near the site along the Snake is a concrete monument, topped with a lion's head, a British symbol. A replica of the fort can be visited in Parma.

The Hudson's Bay Fort Boise should not be confused with the Fort Boise in what is today Boise, Idaho. That fort was also called Boise Barracks. This U.S. Army fort was established by Oregon and Washington Army volunteers in July 1863 to protect Oregon Trail emigrants and miners who were flocking to the gold mines of Idaho. It was the base of operations during General George Crook's campaign against the Snake Indians (1866-1868) and General O.O. Howard's war with the Bannock Indians in 1878.

Fort Boise Activity

Although Fort Boise was later used to supply the pioneers, it was first built to help with the fur trade.

Research the colors of these animals and color them the proper colors. Using the animal names from the list, label the furbearing animals that were often trapped in the West.

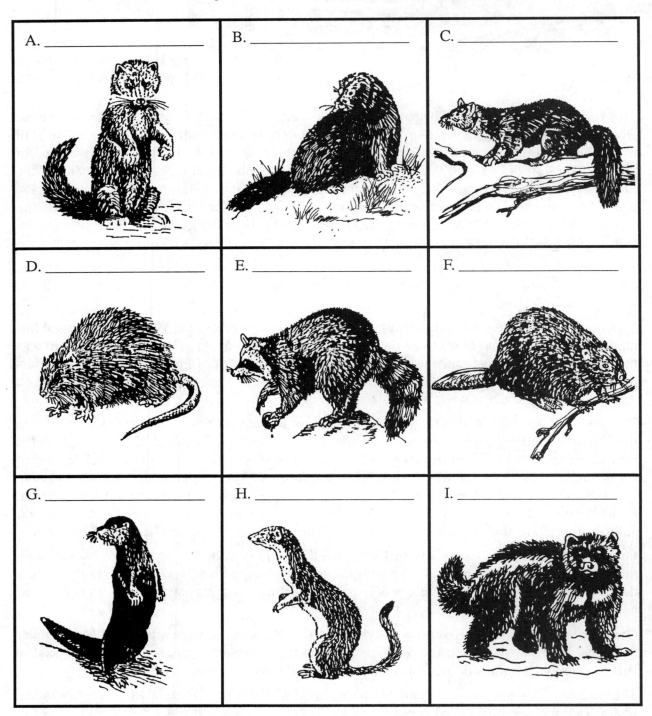

A. _____

B. _____

C. _____

D. _____

E. _____

F. _____

G. _____

H. _____

I. _____

Top Hat

One reason fur traders traveled to the West was for the beaver furs that could be sold to make top hats. This type of hat, also called the stovepipe hat, was the fashion of the day for men.

54

Eastern Oregon

Vale, Huntington, Baker City, OR
Malheur and Baker Counties

Vale Area
Malheur County

At *Keeney Historic Site* (Lytle Pass) the Bureau of Land Management has a display area beside a half mile (.8 km) of well-worn wagon ruts. Osborn Cross wrote on August 30, 1849: ". . . road led up through the hills by a narrow gorge for about four or five miles . . . looked as if it had been intended for a public highway."

The Grave of John Henderson lies one mile (1.6 km) south of Vale. On August 9, 1852, he died of thirst, unaware that he was within sight of the Malheur River. Further back on the trail his team of animals had died. He (and a friend) had to continue on foot, carrying their few possessions. The twenty miles (32 km) separating the Snake and Malheur Rivers was too great a struggle.

The *Malheur River* at Vale was often mentioned in pioneer journals because of its hot springs. John C. Fremont wrote on October 12, 1843: "My attention was attracted by smoke on the right side of the river . . . the water was 193 degrees. The ground, which was too hot for the naked foot, was covered . . . with an incrustation of common salt, very white and good, and fine grained."

Farewell Bend
SE corner of Baker County on I-84 near Huntington, OR

The pioneers had been following the Snake River for about 330 miles (531 km) since Fort Hall. Farewell Bend was an important landmark to them because this was their last view of the Snake. Cecilia Emily McMillen wrote on August 24, 1852: "Came to Snake River for the last time. Here it runs between lofty . . . mountains. So farewell Snake."

Flagstaff Hill
5 miles (8 km) NE of Baker City, OR on Highway 86

When the pioneers crossed over this hill, they had just passed through a terrible stretch of barren, rocky trail. Here, they got their first glimpse of the lush beauty and promise that lay ahead. The view was the Oregon they had imagined. It has been said that the optimists saw the magnificent Baker Valley below and the pessimists saw the towering Blue Mountains looming ahead.

The National Historic Oregon Trail Interpretive Center, run by the Bureau of Land Management, is located on Flagstaff Hill. It is an extensive re-creation of life on the trail. Six major subjects are covered: The Oregon Trail, mining, natural history, Native American contacts, trappers and traders, and the General Land Office's role in settling the West. Paths lead to Oregon Trail ruts. The BLM wants to keep the view of the trail as much like what the emigrants experienced as possible.

Ezra Meeker

Ezra Meeker placed a monument marking the Oregon Trail in downtown Baker City in 1906 (although the trail is really about 5 miles [8.05 km] away). Meeker said, "In one place [Baker City] eight hundred school children contributed their mites [coins] to place a bronze tablet on the granite shaft erected by the citizens as a 'children's offering' to the memory of the pioneers." In 1852 he had been an emigrant with his wife and baby and then in 1906, at age 75, he retraced the trip in reverse. With flowing white hair and beard, Meeker again traveled by an ox-drawn covered wagon. He traveled east to interest people along the Oregon Trail route in the importance of saving and marking the trail. When he reached Ohio, he made this speech: "Most of you wonder why a man at this time of life would cross the plain with an ox team at this age of the world and spend fifteen months in so doing when he could have come by rail all the way in five days, surrounded by all the comforts of life. I will tell you why . . . To perpetuate the identity of the old Oregon Trail, to honor the true heroes who made it, and to kindle in the . . . rising generation a gleam of patriotic sentiment this expedition was undertaken . . . twenty-two monuments of enduring stone have been provided for by the people along the Trail, and most of them are now in place to stand guard for centuries, and to the end that the memory of the old Trail shall not fall into oblivion and be forgotten by the generations to come."

Much of the trail had been destroyed, and he was worried that this piece of American history would soon be gone. He told people that their parents and grandparents had helped make the trail but that the past was being forgotten. He described what was happening to the trail: "We could find traces of it here and there, and then lose it. Part had been fenced up, the fields plowed, and all visible signs gone. In other places nature had been at work. The storms of a half century have changed the face of the country, the river crossings and other landmarks, by growth of vegetation and otherwise. Then again, cities have been built over it, great irrigation ditches have been dug . . . ."

Through his travels and the many books he wrote, he sparked new interest in the trail. A book written from his journal, *Ox-Team Days on the Oregon Trail*, was popular for many years. In 1907, at the end of his trip, he even drove his covered wagon to the White House and was honored by President Theodore Roosevelt!

Ezra Meeker traveled many parts of the trail over his life, but the trips listed below show that they were made using different methods of transportation.

1852 Traveled in a covered wagon from east to west as a young man to start a new life for his family (and returned by train)

1902 Traveled in a covered wagon from west to east as an elderly man to help people remember this pioneer route

1915 Traveled in a car over parts of the trail that could be reached by car

1924 Traveled part of the route by airplane

1928 After trying to again travel the trail from east to west, at age 98, he became ill and went to a hospital in Detroit. He traveled home to Puyallup by train. A few months later he died on December 3, 1928.

GA1473

Eastern Oregon Activity

Imagine that you were Ezra Meeker. Write a journal entry for three of his five Oregon Trail trips. You must do 1852 and the route east in 1906. Then you may choose between his later travels by car, airplane, or train. Be sure to put a date on each journal page and write a good description of what he might have seen and felt on each of the days. Tell how things had changed during the years between his trips. In order to make your writing realistic, you might have to do some research on what life was like during those years.

Blue Mountains

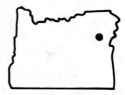

Hilgard Junction State Park

6 ½ miles (10.5 km) west of La Grande, Oregon, Union County

Northeastern Oregon

Today's "B" Street in La Grande follows the Oregon Trail route. Here the trail climbed out of the Grande Ronde ("Great Circle") Valley. On the west side of the hill there had been many wagon ruts and rope-burned trees left from lowering the wagons down the steep hill. This pioneer evidence has now been destroyed by logging. The pioneers camped near what is today Hilgard State Park and nearby Pioneer Springs. Most pioneers arrived in this section of the mountains in early fall when millions of huckleberries were ripe. Many pies were made and the berries were often mentioned in pioneer diaries.

As the pioneers started west from Hilgard, they started the very difficult climb into the Blue Mountains. Jesse Applegate, a 7-year-old pioneer of 1843 (whose famous uncle, also Jesse, led the expedition's livestock), remembered the climb: "The timber had to be cut and removed to make a way for the wagons . . . we were overtaken by a snowstorm which made the prospect very dismal. I remember wading through mud and snow and suffering from the cold and wet."

Emigrant Springs

3 miles (5 km) NW of Mecham, Oregon, Umatilla County

In pioneer days, this was a popular camping spot due to the good spring water and grass for the cattle. The spring was supposed to have been discovered by Reverend Jason Lee in 1834, the first missionary to come to the Oregon Country. Highway and pipeline construction have destroyed most of the original spring area, but a damp swale can be seen under the trees south of the park entrance.

The Oregon Trail plaque, mounted on a boulder, was dedicated in person by President Harding. The plaque says: "Dedicated to the memory of the intrepid pioneers who came with the first wagon train in 1843 over the Old Oregon Trail and saved the Oregon Country to the United States . . . Dedicated by Warren G. Harding, President of the United States July 3, 1923."

Deadman Pass

Rest area off I-84 SE of Pendleton, Oregon, Umatilla County

Oregon Trail pioneers passed through this site. Today, a short trail from the rest area parking lot leads to a fenced area of wagon ruts. The colorful name, Deadman Pass, came about after the pioneer days, during the Bannock Indian War of 1878.

When the emigrants finally got through the Blue Mountains, they breathed a sigh of relief. They felt the worst was over. All along their journey, the wagon train captains had been continually pushing them to move quickly. They didn't want to arrive so late in the fall that they would be caught in early snowfalls in the mountains. They often found snow along the passes but it wasn't always falling. Some pioneers made it without having to fight snow and some didn't. In 1844 Rev. Parish wrote that "the rains ceased during the night and this morning it was cloudy. Glad we escaped the Blue Mts. as they are white with snow."

GA1473

Blue Mountains Activity

The pioneers faced many difficult weather conditions on their trip West. There were high winds, scorching summer temperatures, drenching rains, and heavy snowfalls. Putting up with dusty trails, flooded rivers, deep mud, and steep snowy mountains challenged the pioneers.

Imagine you were a pioneer who crossed the forests of the Blue Mountains in a snowstorm. Using crayons on dark-blue construction paper, color a picture of what you saw. Press very hard with your crayons. Prepare the special solution that is found in the recipe below. Brush this watery solution over your entire paper. When it dries, you will see a frosty scene, much like the pioneers might have experienced.

Recipe:
Mix together approximately one part Epsom salts and two parts water. Occasionally, this solution does not give a frosted effect. If this happens, try different proportions of the solution, such as equal parts of both salt and water. Paint over the paper again. It is best to mix the solution the night before because Epsom salts take a long time to dissolve.

This frosty scene appears because as the water slowly evaporates from the solution, the Epsom salts molecules move closer together. They line up in an orderly pattern and form long needle-shaped crystals. The shape of the crystal is determined by the shape of the molecules as they stack together like building blocks.

Many pioneers found snow on the Blue Mountains. Enjoy folding and cutting out six-sided snowflakes like the pioneers might have seen and making a bulletin board with your class.

Materials:
squares of paper—white or silver
scissors

What to Do:
1. Fold the square of paper on the diagonal.

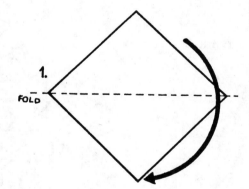

2. Fold again as shown in 2 through 5.

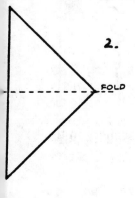
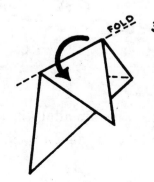
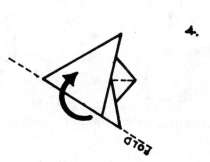
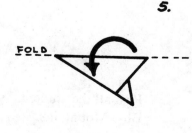

GA1473

6. Cut off the top of the cone, using a zigzag or wavy line.

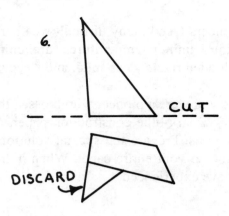

CUT

DISCARD

7. Make some cuts on the sides of the cone but don't cut all the way across.

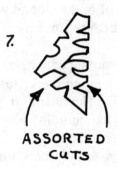

ASSORTED CUTS

8. Unfold and you have a 6-sided snowflake.

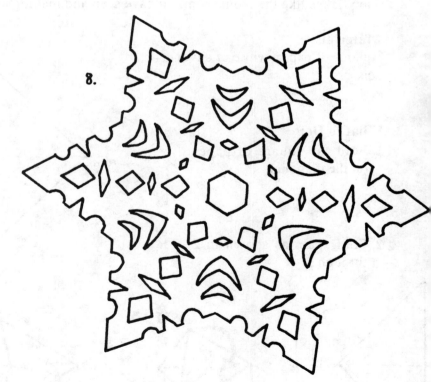

Post all the students' snowflakes on a bulletin board depicting the beautiful winter scenery in the Blue Mountains.

GA147

Whitman Mission
1836-1847

On February 18, 1836, the day after their wedding, Narcissa and Marcus Whitman said good-bye to their families and friends and began their emigrant journey West. At their request they were being sent by the American Board of Foreign Missions, a society supported by several Protestant churches, to bring the Christian religion to the Indians. Interest in the Oregon Country started in the 1820s with an article in a New York Methodist publication which described the visit to St. Louis by some Western Indians

Whitman Mission
National Historic Site
Walla Walla, Washington
Walla Walla County

seeking teachers and the white man's "Book of heaven"–the Bible. This mostly fictional story stimulated interest in missionary work among Oregon Indians. Going along with the Whitmans were Eliza and Henry Spalding. Their supplies were loaded in a covered wagon. A wagon like this had never made it further than Fort Laramie but the Whitmans hoped to prove it could be done. They believed that if others knew of their success, they would be encouraged to join the Whitmans at their frontier settlement. Along the journey their wagon had to be cut down into a smaller cart, but it was the first vehicle to travel as far west as Fort Boise. The Whitmans were making history. At that time, except for a few fur trappers, only Indians lived in the Oregon Country. Narcissa and Eliza were the first pioneer women to cross the Rocky Mountains.

Whitman Mission

GA1473

Marcus Whitman

Narcissa Whitman

In November 1836, the Whitmans finally reached Waiilatpu (wy-eel-at-poo), a Cayuse Indian word for "the people of the place of the rye grass," where they would build their mission. It was a beautiful clearing on the Walla Walla River. The Spaldings built their mission 110 miles (177 km) to the east at Lapwai among the Nez Perce Indians near today's Lewiston, Idaho. Narcissa and Eliza missed each other. They had a pact that every morning at 9:00 they would stop what they were doing, read scriptures from the Bible, and pray for the children of the world. For the next eleven years, Marcus and Narcissa worked among the Cayuse Indians. Narcissa taught in the mission school while Marcus conducted church services, practiced medicine, and taught the Indians the basics of farming. For part of each year the Indians went away to the bison country, the camas meadows, and the salmon fisheries in search of food. Whitman realized that the mission could not fulfill its purpose if the Indians remained nomadic. He therefore encouraged them to be farmers but with little success. Marcus was generally successful as a doctor treating the Indians but was not successful converting them to Christianity.

In 1842 when the mission board ordered the closing of many of its Oregon missions, Marcus Whitman made a heroic trip east and persuaded the board to reverse its decision. Preparing to return to Oregon in May 1843, he found nearly 1000 people gathered on the banks of the Kansas River, ready to emigrate west. Whitman acted as a doctor and guide to the "Great Migration" of 1843, encouraging the pioneers to move quickly to avoid the winter snows. Jesse Applegate wrote: "Whitman's constant advice, which we knew was based on a knowledge of the road before us, was, 'Travel, travel, travel; nothing else will take you to the end of your journey; nothing is wise that does not help you along; nothing is good for you that causes a moment's delay.'" He led the first wagons all the way to the Columbia River. Whitman had more to do with the settling of Oregon than any other, for he showed that wagons could cross the continent. Many pioneers started West and the mission became a welcome stopping-off point for tired travelers, especially in 1843 and 1844. A more direct trail was built in later years, but pioneers needing help continued to go to the mission for food, blacksmithing, lodging, or medical help.

The Whitman's daughter, Alice Clarissa, was born at Waiilatpu on March 14, 1837, three months after Narcissa arrived. She was the first white American child born in the Oregon Country. She was only two years old when she took a cup from the table and went down to the Walla Walla River to get a drink. She fell into the water and drowned. The Whitmans were heartbroken and to ease the hurt eventually adopted eleven orphans. The seven Sager children, whose parents had died on the trail, were left to be raised by the Whitmans in 1844. Also living at the mission were the daughters of former fur trappers, Mary Ann Bridger, daughter of Jim Bridger, and Helen Meek, daughter of Joe Meek.

The Whitmans and Cayuse learned from one another for a while. Then their differences became too great and their life together ended in tragedy. The Cayuse began to view the many emigrants with alarm. The Indians began to suspect that the whites had not come to preach to them but instead to take permanent control of their hunting grounds. To make matters even worse, in the fall of 1847 a group of emigrants brought measles with them. Some of the white children at the mission caught the disease and were cured in a few days by Dr. Whitman. The Cayuse had no resistance to most of the diseases of the whites and they didn't get well. Four or five Indian children died each day, and by the middle of November half of the 350 tribe members had died. The Cayuse saw the white children getting well and their people dying. According to the custom of the Cayuse tribe, any "medicine man" who failed to stop death might himself need to be killed. By tribal rumor, Dr. Whitman was causing sickness on purpose, poisoning the Indian children even as he pretended to treat them, in order to make room for more emigrants. He had to be stopped. Dr Whitman tried desperately to relieve the suffering but his efforts were in vain.

On November 29, 1847, a band of Cayuse attacked the mission and killed Marcus and Narcissa Whitman, John and Francis Sager, and nine others. A few survivors escaped, but about fifty people, mostly women and children, were taken captive. Two young girls, Louisa Sager, Helen Mar Meek, and a small boy died from the measles. The Indians burned the mission buildings and cut down all of the trees in the orchard. When settlers down the Columbia River heard of the massacre, Peter Skene Ogden of the Hudson's Bay Company arranged for the captives to be ransomed. The ransom was 62 blankets, 63 cotton shirts, 12 guns, 600 loads of ammunition, 37 pounds (17 kg) of tobacco, and 12 flints. The pioneer militia of about 500 men chased the Cayuse into the mountains. The chase lasted for two years, off and on. Then, to buy peace for the tribe, five Cayuse warriors gave themselves up. All five were tried and hung as punishment for the massacre. Protestant missionary work among the Oregon Indians ended with the massacre.

63

Joe Meek, a retired mountain man, rode his horse all the way to Washington, D.C., in the winter of 1847 to carry news of the tragedy and petitions from settlers. Meek arrived on May 28, 1848, ragged, whiskered, and still wearing his trail-stained buckskins. Without bothering to change his clothes, he went to the White House steps and demanded to see his cousin-in-law, President James Polk to tell him the story of the massacre. Meek was able to speak to Congress, giving a sensational report of the need for Oregon to become an official U.S. Territory so it could have protection for the settlers. On August 14, 1848, Congress granted territorial status for Oregon (including Washington and parts of Idaho), the first formal territorial government west of the Rockies.

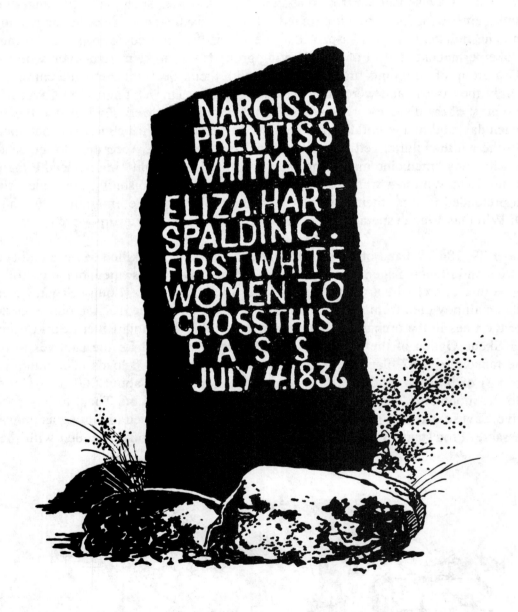

This monument is at South Pass in Wyoming.

GA147

Whitman Mission Activity

People in the East often dreamed of life on a farm in Oregon's fertile Willamette Valley. They learned about the Oregon Country in many ways but often through letters that were sent back home by the emigrants. For example, the letters of the Whitmans, widely published after their deaths, spread information about life in the West. Here are some examples.

A letter from Dr. Marcus Whitman, written in September, 1843, gives a good picture of life at the Whitman Mission. In this part, he writes about the seasonal life of the Cayuse Indians.

". . . The latter part of June is the usual period for buffalo hunters to set out on their expedition. A migration of from 40 to 60 miles takes them across the Blue Mountains into the Grand Ronde. The river of the Grand Ronde is well supplied with fish and the mountains abound with bear and deer. The wheat harvest, which begins the latter part of July, and the care of their other crops, bring many to the station, who remain till the first of October or until the potato harvest is past. During this period there are more in the neighborhood of the station than at any other period except the spring. Our congregation averages from 50 to 200. During this period their attention is divided between their crops and herds, hunting, fishing, and preparing dried fruit. Soon after the potatoes are secured they disperse to their winter quarters. From 50 to 60 remain during the winter . . . ."

Narcissa Whitman described life on the Oregon Trail in one of her letters:

". . .While the horses are feeding we get breakfast in a hurry and eat it. By this time the words, 'Catch up! Catch up!' ring through the camp for moving. We are ready to start usually at six, travel till eleven, encamp, rest and feed, and start again about two; travel until six, or better . . . then encamp for the night. Tell mother I am a very good housekeeper on the prairie. I wish she could just take a peep at us while we are sitting at meals. Our table is the ground, our table-cloth is an India-rubber cloth, used when it rains as a cloak; our dishes are made of tin . . . Let me assure you of this, we relish our food none the less for sitting on the ground while eating. We have tea and a plenty of milk, which is a luxury in this country."

Imagine you are a pioneer now living in the Oregon Country. Write a letter back to your relatives in the East, describing life in your new home or describing your journey to Oregon. Be accurate with the facts you should know—what the land looked like, climate, locations, historical accuracy, and so forth. Your characters can, of course, be fictional. You will be writing in a historical fiction style.

GA1473

The Sager Family Story

In the fall of 1844 the seven orphaned Sager children arrived at the Whitman Mission. They were accepted into the home of Marcus and Narcissa Whitman. Many children lost their parents on the Oregon trail, but for three years, until the massacre of 1847, the Sager family knew the Whitmans like no one else ever did, as their parents. The story of their experiences has fascinated people ever since.

The Sager children's journey to the Whitman Mission started in Missouri in the spring of 1844 when they started across the Oregon Trail with their parents, Henry and Naomi Sager. The children were John, 13; Francis, 12; Catherine (Katie), 10; Elizabeth, 8; Matilda Jane, 6; and Hannah Louisa, 3. Henrietta Louise was born soon after the trip began. There were many problems along the way. Near Fort Laramie, Catherine fell while trying to jump from a wagon. She caught her dress on the axle and broke her leg. After leaving Fort Laramie, Henry Sager became sick with mountain fever. They traveled on through South Pass but he died along the Green River. Without her husband, Naomi had a big job with seven children. A few weeks after her husband's death, Mrs. Sager also died. Before she died, she asked that the children be taken to the Whitman Mission.

When they reached the Whitman Mission, their aunt Sally Shaw washed them and had them put on their best clothes. As she took them to meet the Whitmans, Aunt Sally cried and said, "I wonder what will be the fate of you little orphan children." The Whitmans agreed to keep the children until spring. If by that time either the Sagers or the Whitmans weren't happy with the arrangement, the children would be brought to their uncle and guardian, Capt. William Shaw, in the Willamette Valley. The arrangement proved to work well and the children were able to stay together. Later, the Whitmans legally adopted them but let them keep their Sager family name.

Years later, Matilda Jane told about life at the Whitman Mission: "I wish I could give you a picture of the Whitman Mission—of the family life of the Whitmans, of the morning and evening prayers, of the work with the Indians, of the emigrants . . . of the bathing in the river in the summer, of our walks with Mrs. Whitman, of the gathering of wildflowers, of our simple meals, of driving the cows to pasture, of the routine of work and all the rest of it . . . She [Narcissa] had the New England idea of strict discipline, and there was no danger of any of us becoming spoiled. She was a good woman, and Dr. Whitman was a man you could not help respecting and admiring."

Following the massacre (see page 63), the four remaining Sager children and others were held captive for a month. John and Francis had died in the massacre. In the confusion of the massacre, Louisa did not receive proper care for her measles and died. A ransom was paid for the release of the captives by Peter Skene Ogden. Ogden took them to Fort Walla Walla, the Hudson's Bay Company post. From there they went in open boats to Fort Vancouver, down the swift Columbia River, during very cold weather. They enjoyed their comfortable three days at

66

GA1473

the fort, and the girls were excited about the prospect of being adopted by some of the families there. When Ogden was asked about the adoptions, he refused them saying that it was his intention not to leave them with the British but to keep the children together and deliver them to "the American governor's hands without fail." They then started for Oregon City by boat. Along the way, at Portland, a lot of men had come down to the dock and when they saw them coming, fired a salute. The children tried to hide in the bottom of the boat, thinking they were trying to kill them. They were reassured that the guns were only being fired in their honor. The children's story was well known and the men cheered for them. When Peter Skene Ogden stepped ashore in Portland which, at that time, was a town of only two frame houses and a few log cabins, he was greeted by George Abernethy, the provisional governor of Oregon. An American flag was flying. Ogden presented Abernethy with papers and then turned to the group of freed captives and said, "Now you are a free people. You can go where you please."

It would be nice to think that the Sagers' troubles were over at last and that kind friends took them in and kept them together like the Whitmans had done. This did not happen. The Oregon settlers were mostly poor, had many children of their own, and were struggling to make new lives for themselves. A family might be able to take in one child but not four! The children were separated and never again lived together. Life was hard for most of them.

In 1921, Matilda Jane Sager Delaney told of her difficult experiences of being taken to live with a family on a farm near Forest Grove: "They lived in a one room cabin. All the cooking was done in the fireplace. Sometimes the coals did not last overnight, so I would be sent a mile or more to a neighbor's to get a shovelful of hot coals to rebuild the fire." The husband of the family was very harsh and intolerant. "For several years I was never without welts or black and blue marks from constant beatings. I remember once he was going away on a trip. He told me to go and cut a thick switch. I thought he wanted it for his horse, as he was saddling up. I brought the switch. He called to me and, seizing me by the shoulder, gave me an unmerciful beating. I said, 'What have I done?' He said, 'You haven't done anything. I am going away. The chances are you will do something to deserve a beating while I am gone, and I won't be here to give it to you, so I will see to my duty before leaving.'" The husband had gone to the gold fields in California and the wife made money by knitting wool into socks. Matilda had to help support the family, but it was another horrible experience: "The winter was cold and the sheep died or were frozen to death. It was my job to pull the wool off the sheep that died and wash it in the creek. Doing the family washing in the stream by beating the clothes with a paddle on a log and rinsing them in the cold water was hard, but washing the dirt and grease out of that wool was a job that was heartbreaking for a little girl nine years old . . . Childhood was a time of terror and bitterness when I was a girl." She was whipped so much that the neighbors finally complained and her case was being considered by a judge. "While they were settling that I married a miner from Shasta County, California, and went to the gold mines with him. He was 31 and I was 15." Over the years, she had three husbands and eight children.

Catherine, at age sixteen, married Clark Pringle and had eight children. They also took in seven-year-old Henrietta, who was considered a burden to the people she was living with because she was too young to do much work. Five years later, Henrietta went with her Uncle Solomon to travel as an entertainer in mining towns. Clark had told her that mining camps were rough, wild, and dirty, and no place for a young girl. She ignored his protests and went to California, marrying twice before she died at age 26. Someone had a grudge against her husband and shot at him, but the bullet missed and killed Henrietta instead. She apparently had no children. Elizabeth married at age eighteen to William Helm and they had nine children.

67

On the fiftieth anniversary of the Whitman Massacre in 1897, Matilda, Catherine, and Elizabeth, now elderly ladies, with other massacre survivors, were invited to be honored guests at the dedication of a monument on the site of the Whitman Mission. The women felt pride and happiness. They had worked hard for the day the Whitmans would be honored with a monument recognizing their accomplishments. The monument, a tall marble shaft pointing to the sky, still stands today on a hill above the mission site. In 1940 the grounds became the Whitman Mission National Historic Site, visited by thousands of tourists each year. Archaeologists had studied and marked the mission buildings. Visitors can see the "Great Grave" of those who were killed, plus see the grave of baby Alice. There is also a museum with displays showing both the pioneer and Indian ways of life.

Although the story of the Sager family is now told accurately at museums and in some books, other books continue to tell the story in an inaccurate, distorted way. The true story is amazing and fascinating. It seems strange that some authors would think it would be more interesting if they changed the truth. The surviving Sager girls wanted the story of their family told accurately. In 1926, Matilda's daughter, Sarah Naomi Swan, told her about an article about the Sager family that had been written in the January issue of *Cosmopolitan* magazine by Honoré Morrow. This article claimed that after the deaths of the Sager parents the children were left without adult help and were forced to continue alone. It contained a ridiculous description of Catherine with her broken leg, who she mistakenly called Matilda, riding on the back of a sick cow. Supposedly they staggered alone, half-starved, across sagebrush deserts and over the Blue Mountains to the Whitman Mission. This would have been impossible and just didn't happen. Instead, the children were very well cared for on the trip. This was an insult to the Sagers. Over the years the girls kept in contact with Dr. Degen and the Shaws, people who had helped them when their parents died, visiting them when they could and writing them letters.

Matilda was furious at Honoré Morrow and wrote her, "I positively forbid you to use either the name of Sager and its family history. I do not feel pleased or gratified by your story in the *Cosmopolitan*, quite the contrary." She said she would have helped give her the true account if she had wished. Mrs. Morrow, though, ignored the letter. Later that year her book, *On to Oregon!* (now sometimes known as *Seven Alone*), was published. Some of the mistakes had been corrected but others were added. The story in her book spread for years in other books, articles, movies, and on television. Matilda fought the false story the rest of her life.

The Sager Family Story Activity

Here's a challenge for you. You are a historian trying to correct the errors in books and movies about the Sager family. Read books listed in the bibliography of this guide, especially by the authors C. Shields, N. Frazier, and F. Lockley and any other books that will tell you the true story. Compare these accounts of the Sager story with those found in other books and movies. List the errors you find and also list the true facts. Example:

1. False information and source
   "Dr. Dutch looked at him not unkindly but very doubtfully." Source: *Seven Alone* p. 78

True, corrected information
This was not his name. Although many spelling variations can be found, the name was closer to Dr. Degen.

The Dalles

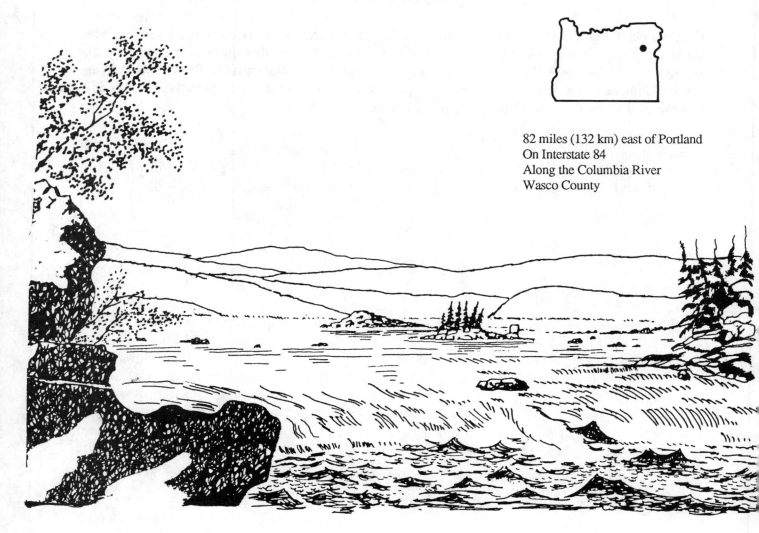

82 miles (132 km) east of Portland
On Interstate 84
Along the Columbia River
Wasco County

From 1838 to 1847 the Wascopam Methodist Mission was at the future site of The Dalles. John C. Fremont wrote in 1843 ". . . encamped near the mission . . . hospitable and kind reception . . . two good-looking wooden dwelling houses, and a large school house, with stables, barn, and garden, and large cleared fields between the houses and the river bank, on which were scattered the wooden huts of an Indian village . . . ." The mission served as a stopping point for emigrants. William H. McNeil wrote in 1843, "The Methodist Missionaries here gave (the emigrants) a warm greeting and provided some fresh meats and other foods . . . ."

Fort Dalles, a military post, was established here in 1850. It housed two companies of the Regiment of Mounted Riflemen. Its purpose was to protect emigrant traffic on the Oregon Trail. By 1852 the town of The Dalles had grown up around the post.

In French, "The Dalles" means "slabs," named for a deep, swift chute in the river caused by basalt rocks that made dangerous waterfalls, currents, and whirlpools. Today, large dams make the river look smooth and make water travel easy. However, in pioneer days, the river was very dangerous. Just west of The Dalles, emigrants started this often frightening raft trip down the river. There was no way for the wagons to continue on down the riverbank. This was where the Cascade Mountains reached the river. They could have walked the slippery, wet riverbank trail if they wanted to move only their livestock, but wagons could not get through.

When the emigrants reached The Dalles, they had a difficult decision to make. They could float their wagons on rafts down the dangerous Columbia River to Fort Vancouver or they could take the steep route around Mt. Hood to Oregon City. This final part of the trail, no matter which route, was the most dangerous and difficult segment of the 2000-mile (3220-km) journey. It was also at a time when food was running low, people and animals were near exhaustion, and illness was common. John C. Fremont in 1843 described the many emigrant families with their "thin and insufficient clothing, bare-headed and barefooted children attesting to the length of the journey." This portion of the trip also had to be done during the fall months which could be sheer misery with cold gusty winds, drenching rains, and even early snowstorms.

It was expensive, time-consuming, and hard work to get ready to raft down the river. Pioneers had to cut 40-foot (12.2-m) logs to build rafts. Sometimes they hired men from Fort Vancouver or Indians to paddle them downstream in large dugout canoes or by bateaux, a flat-bottom boat. It was very expensive to hire this transportation, so often they traded oxen or other goods to help pay their fares. Indians also controlled some of the necessary portages where the rapids blocked the route. Emigrants had to get out and walk at the portages and the Indians asked to be paid for giving their skillful help. The lack of boats caused long delays which were very costly to the one hundred or more people usually stranded at The Dalles. With good connections at the six or seven portages, the float to Fort Vancouver could be made in one or two days, but usually it took three days.

In November of 1843, John C. Fremont wrote about traveling the Cascades part of the Columbia River near the present-day town of Cascade Locks which had the most dangerous rapids: ". . . the river forms a great cascade with a series of rapids . . . breaking over . . . masses of rocks leaving a handsome bay to the right, with several rocky, pine-covered islands . . . halted . . . where there were several Indian huts, and where our guide signified it was customary to hire Indians to assist in making the portage . . . the water being white with foam among ugly rocks, and boiling into a thousand whirlpools." Some emigrants, like James Nesmith, found this water route exciting. While his supplies were being portaged, he sat on a rock reading Shakespeare! (By 1851 steamboat service was available between The Dalles and these Cascade rapids.)

Many emigrants faced the horror of watching members of their families drown in the rapids. Jesse Applegate recalled his family's tragedy: "We had an Indian pilot . . . As we approached this bend I could hear the sound of rapids, and presently the boat began to rise and fall and rock from side to side . . . I began to think this was no ordinary rapid . . . when looking across the river I saw a smaller boat about opposite to us near the south bank. The persons in the boat were . . . [2 men] and 3 boys: Elisha Applegate, aged about eleven, and Warren and Edward Applegate, each about nine years old . . . . This boat now near the south shore, it would seem, should have followed our boat as the pilot was with us, and this was a dangerous part of the river . . . presently there was a wail of anguish, a shriek, and a scene of confusion in our boat that no language can describe. The boat we were watching disappeared and we saw the men and boys struggling in the water. (The adults) seeing their children drowning, were seizing with frenzy, and dropping their oars sprang up from their seats and were about to leap from the boat to make a desperate attempt to swim to them, when mother and Aunt Cynthia, in voices that were distinctly heard above the roar of the rushing waters . . . brought them to a realization of our own perilous situation, and the madness of an attempt to reach the other side of the river by swimming." One man and the two youngest Applegate boys drowned in the capsized boat. The loss of their sons was a crushing experience for Jesse and Lindsay Applegate. By 1846, these two well-known Oregon pioneers, with others, blazed a new trail into western Oregon from the south.

GA1473

In September of 1845, Samuel Barlow arrived at The Dalles. He quickly decided that, after six months of bumping across the plains, his battered wagon wasn't worth the $50 fee that would be charged to float it down the river. That year there was a "traffic jam" of sorts and they would have had to wait weeks for a boat. They also couldn't afford the high price of food for themselves and their stock. He heard rumors of an Indian trail that crossed the Cascade barrier south of Mt. Hood. He also remembered seeing a notch on Mt. Hood as he had come from the east. He decided he could cross the mountains rather than float down the Columbia. People thought he was crazy to try this route but Barlow told them, "God never made a mountain but what He provided a place for man to go over or around it."

Barlow was joined by some other emigrants and with thirty wagons they started around the south side of Mt. Hood. It was a hard journey and they had to leave their wagons stuck in the mountains over the winter. In order to rescue the wagons the next spring, Barlow got permission from Oregon's Provisional Government to build a road into the Cascades. In addition to rescuing his wagons, Barlow built a new route from The Dalles to Oregon City. This new Barlow Road opened as a toll road in 1846. The emigrants now had a choice. They could travel over a difficult, steep mountain "trail" on the Barlow Road or they could float down the dangerous Columbia River.

Samuel Barlow

GA1473

The Dalles Activity

If the pioneers could not find guides to float their families and wagons down the Columbia River, rafts would have to be built. This was a difficult project when it was often cold, windy, and rainy and they were tired and hungry.

Build a miniature raft or some type of simple boat out of sticks. Real sticks would be the most realistic, as if they were logs, but you could also use Popsicle™ sticks. The raft will need long oars to be used for steering. Make it strong but see if you can use materials you think the pioneers would have had. Be sure this raft would be the right shape to hold a wagon and some passengers. Usually the wheels were removed from a wagon during the float trip and the wagon bed set flat on the raft.

Place your raft in a basin of water. Use your hand to swirl around the water to create rapids. (You could also use the faucet or a hose to make the rapids.) Is your raft constructed so it will stay together and not tip over? If you put a wagon model on top, will the wagon be secure enough to stay on?

After you have experimented with your raft in the water, write a description of an experience on the Columbia River, as if you were a pioneer. Remember how Jesse Applegate recalled the tragedy his family experienced on the river and how John C. Fremont described the rapids? Those can give you some ideas for your writing. Here are two more pioneer descriptions of boat trips down the Columbia:

Samuel Parker in mid-October of 1845 wrote, "I did not expect to get to the city with my fore sick children and my oldest girl that was sick. I was loking at the time for her to die. I tuck my seat in the canoe by her and held her up and the same at nite when I come to the cascade falls. I had to make portage of 3 miles, I put my sick girl in a blanket and pack her & only rested once that day. We maid the portage with the help of my fore Indians . . . ."

Pioneer Ezra Meeker said that after the terrible trials of the Snake River and then the canyons and dusty deserts of Oregon, the emigrants were so tired that when they finally got on the rafts, they sat exhausted and in silence. He said that suddenly someone started singing "Home, Sweet Home." Soon everyone was singing and "men found themselves sobbing like babies."

Ezra Meeker

GA1473

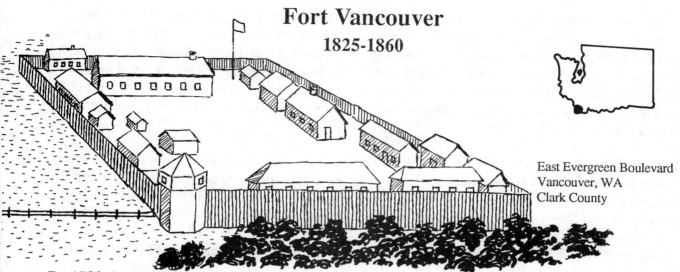

Fort Vancouver
1825-1860

East Evergreen Boulevard
Vancouver, WA
Clark County

By 1790 the United States and Great Britain began to have interests in claiming the North American land along the north Pacific coast and trading with the Indians. Explorers were sent by ship and overland to look for the valuable sea otters and beavers for furs, to find travel routes, to meet the Indians, and to establish claims to the area. Trapping companies began to arrive. The biggest was the Hudson's Bay Company (HBC) from London, England.

The Hudson's Bay Company set up many forts but the most important was Fort Vancouver, located about 100 miles (161 km) upstream from the mouth of the Columbia River. In the early 1800s, the United States and Great Britain were each struggling to control this region. By 1818, under the Joint Occupancy Agreement, the two countries agreed to share what was then called the Oregon Country until they could later decide on a boundary. The vast area that the Hudson's Bay Company controlled was known as the Columbia Department (or the Oregon Country). At that time it extended from the Rocky Mountains to the Pacific Ocean and from Russian Alaska to Spanish California (Mexico). Today, this area consists of Oregon, Washington, Idaho, the western parts of Montana and Wyoming, and the western half of Canada's British Columbia.

The person most responsible for the success of Fort Vancouver was Dr. John McLoughlin. He was the chief factor, the person responsible for the company's business. McLoughlin looked very distinguished, with piercing blue eyes, long flowing white hair, massive chest and broad shoulders, and height of 6'4" (1.93 m). McLoughlin's job was to squeeze the Americans out of the fur trade and to firmly establish the British claim to all of Oregon. He was also to keep peace with the Indians. As long as McLoughlin was in charge, there was peace in the Oregon Country. He knew how to make friends of the Indians of the Columbia. They called him "White-Headed Eagle." He was stern and strict but always fair. He kept his promises.

Fort Vancouver became the fur trading capital of the Pacific coast. It was the largest trading center in the West before the California gold rush. The fort's warehouses stocked supplies for the fur brigades, the Indian and settler trade, and for the twenty to thirty other company forts in the department. Almost all of the trade items were imported from Britain so there was a two-year lapse between ordering and receiving. Trappers brought their furs to exchange for money and supplies. Indians traded furs for beads and tools. Gardens were planted outside its walls to grow food for the company. McLoughlin worked very hard so that the Columbia Department would make a profit. Most days the workers rose at 5:00 a.m. and worked until 6:00 p.m. or later. Fort Vancouver was no place for a lazy person.

GA1473

McLoughlin and the Hudson's Bay Company offered the only "civilization" in the Oregon Country and was the most important settlement. Fort Vancouver was a stockaded fort. Its gates were guarded by tall Scotsmen in kilts. Inside the stockade were about two dozen buildings such as a bakery, a pharmacy, a warehouse, and a store where furs were sold. There were also workshops for mechanics, carpenters, blacksmiths, coopers, tanners, and wheelwrights. They provided these "firsts" in the Pacific Northwest: school, library, hospital, theater, flour mill, lumber mill, and more.

Even though McLoughlin worked for the British Hudson's Bay Company, when the American pioneers came West, he made supplies and credit available to the needy settlers. They didn't have to pay him back until they could get money from their first crops. He also lent them company tools and livestock. He was known for his hospitality and kindness. He befriended Americans even though he knew if many settled in the Oregon Country, the Hudson's Bay Company would have to leave. Time after time he sent out relief expeditions when he heard of stranded wagon trains.

McLoughlin did more to help the American emigrants than any other single person. John Boardman wrote on November 3, 1843, "Fort Vancouver . . . well received by Doct. McLaughlin, who charged nothing for the use of his boat sent up for us, nor for the provisions . . . plenty of salmon and potatoes, furnished us house room and wood free of charge, and was very anxious that all should get through safe."

Dr. John McLoughlin

GA1473

The Hudson's Bay Company felt sure that when there was a boundary settlement, the British would have everything north of the Columbia. Therefore, Americans were encouraged to settle in Oregon City or other parts of the Willamette Valley, south of the Columbia. Many more Americans had come to the Oregon Country than British citizens. The large number of Americans resulted in the division of the Oregon Country in 1846. Instead of the Columbia River becoming the border, it was divided farther north at the 49th parallel, a decision that left Fort Vancouver on American land.

For a few years, the Hudson's Bay Company continued to trade with settlers and Indians. The fur trade was dying out because too many valuable fur-bearing animals had been killed. Also, the fur hat, which had been the men's fashion of the day, was replaced by the silk hat. Fort Vancouver began to rely on the American settlers for business, selling them food, household goods, and seeds. As the settlers began to build their own towns and grow their own food, trade at the fort declined. Fort Vancouver lost its importance. The Hudson's Bay Company moved out in 1860. By 1866 fires, vandalism, and decay had destroyed all the structures. Today, much of the fort has been reconstructed by the National Park Service and can be visited by tourists.

Since McLoughlin had been so helpful to the Americans, he was criticized by much of the Hudson's Bay Company. In 1845, McLoughlin resigned from the Company when he was almost sixty-one years old. He had a fine home built in Oregon City and moved in in 1846. McLoughlin had generously given away much of his land in Oregon City to five churches and a school. However, he was treated poorly by some Oregon government officials and also by some settlers. When he died in 1857, he had had much of his property taken from him and was nearly broke. It was a very sad ending for a man who had been so generous and who had helped save the lives of so many Americans. Later, however, he was recognized for saving Oregon for the United States. In 1907 the Oregon Legislature declared him the "Father of Oregon."

GA1473

Fort Vancouver Activity

The people at Fort Vancouver ate better than emigrants on the trail, but they were limited in their selections of foods. One of the foods baked at the fort was hardbread biscuits. These biscuits were baked in the "Commoners" Bake Shop, and it was reported that the baker was not the best. This is the kind of bread most of the people at the fort got. If you were an "important" person, though, and ate at Dr. John McLoughlin's house, you got better bread.

Try baking these hardbread biscuits. Remember, they were very, very hard. Usually hardbread was soaked in a liquid before eating so teeth wouldn't be broken!

1. Mix two cups (480 ml) of stone-ground flour with one cup (240 ml) of water.

2. Knead the mixture until it is smooth.

3. Sprinkle flour on a smooth surface. Roll the dough flat until it is $\frac{1}{4}$" (.6 cm) thick.

4. Cut the biscuits out with a can or glass that is 3" to 4" (7.62 to 10.16 cm) in diameter.

5. Poke holes in each biscuit with a fork. (This is how water escapes so the biscuits won't be puffy. That was important to the baker at the fort because flat biscuits were easier to store.)

6. Place the biscuits on a floured cookie sheet. Bake them at 400° F (204° C) for about 35 minutes or until they are hard and cooked all the way through.

7. The recipes makes 12 to 15 biscuits.

8. Do a good job of cleaning up and putting everything away.

Dr. John McLoughlin

GA1473

Laurel Hill
On the Slope of Mount Hood

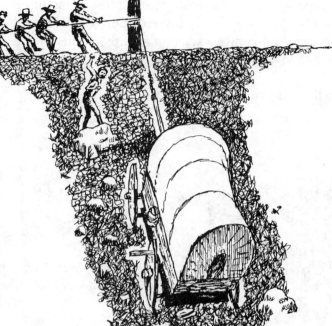

2 ¹/₄ miles (3.6 km) west of Government Camp, Oregon
Highway 26
Clackamas County

Pioneer travels on the Barlow Road, the Mount Hood part of the Oregon Trail, were very hard. This was especially true at Laurel Hill, the steepest part of the entire Oregon Trail and one of the most hazardous.

The pioneers had to lower their wagons 300 feet (91 m) down the steepest part of this 4-mile (6.4-km) hill. Wagons had to go straight down the hill because they were top-heavy and could easily tip over. Laurel Hill was so steep that it was definitely a one-way road west for wagons! It sloped down at a 60 percent grade. (Today, the steepest slope of the Mt. Hood Loop Highway is a 6 percent grade.)

Travel down Laurel Hill was very difficult. Esther Belle Hanna wrote in 1853, "Came to Laurel Hill which is the elephant of these mountains. To give an idea of the descent of this hill would be impossible, for it surpasses anything that I ever saw or heard of for badness." E. W. Conyers described it in 1852 as ". . . something terrible. It is worn down into the soil from 5 to 7 feet, leaving steep banks on both sides, and so narrow that it is almost impossible to walk alongside of the cattle for any distance without leaning against the oxen."

There were several ways pioneers attempted to get their wagons down the hill. Sometimes they combined these approaches:
1. Wagons were slid backwards down the hill with all wheels locked, often by sticking logs through the wagon wheels. A tree was also tied to the rear axle of the wagon and dragging this tree helped with the braking.

2. Some put oxen on the front of the wagon (uphill) to help hold back the wagon and keep it from sliding down too fast. Some animals stumbled and died on the hill. People often helped pull on the wagon with ropes, too, acting as a brake.

3. A rope was tied to the back of the wagon. The rope was also wrapped around a tree at the top of the hill. The rope was gradually let out and the wagon was slowly lowered down. This was called "snubbing." Until a few years ago, rope burns could still be seen on stumps. Sometimes the ropes broke so the wagons crashed and then had to be mended or abandoned.

4. Some pioneers took their wagons apart and slid them down the slope.

Laurel Hill was probably named by the pioneers for the wild rhododendron plants growing there which looked similar to the laurel plant they knew from the East. The plant may also have been confused with the native chinkapin. There was little food for the animals on Mt. Hood. One of Barlow's best horses died from eating this "laurel." Mrs. Barlow wrote, "Poor old Gray is dead, but I hope his meat is good; we will not starve so long as we can eat horse meat." Travel was hard on Mt. Hood but Barlow's daughter, Sara Gaines, wrote jokingly, "We are in the midst of plenty, plenty of wood to make fires, plenty of horses to make meat, plenty of snow to make water, and when it comes to starving, here is your old dog as fat as butter, and he will last us a week."

Traveling down Laurel Hill was very dangerous and difficult for the pioneers. Some men rode backwards down the hill on their wagons in an attempt to help guide them. This was called "riding the tornado." Most women, children, and animals walked down a nearby steep trail. One journal, however, told of a lady who tried to ride down Laurel Hill in her wagon. The ropes broke loose and it is said that "the poor lady had a fit."

Simply walking down the hill could be miserable. Amelia Stewart Knight wrote in her 1853 journal, "It would be useless for me with my pencil to describe the awful road we have just passed over. Let fancy picture a train of wagons and cattle passing through a crooked chimney and we have Big Laurel Hill . . . . We kept as near the road as we could, winding around the fallen timber, sometimes lifting and carrying Chat [a child]. To keep from smelling the carrion [rotting bodies of dead animals], I, as others, holding my nose . . I was sick all night and not able to get out of the wagon in the morning." A few days after experiencing the hardships of Laurel Hill, Mrs. Knight gave birth to her eighth child. No wonder she wasn't feeling well!

GA1473

Laurel Hill Activity

You've read what some of the pioneers said about Laurel Hill. Now you get a chance to write your description of descending down Laurel Hill. In your writing use what you know of the difficulties of pioneer travel on Mount Hood. This description can be from the point of view of a pioneer adult or child, ox, or family dog.

GA1473

Barlow Road Toll Gate

Highway 26–Mt. Hood Loop Highway
½ mile (.8 km) east of Rhododendron, OR
Clackamas County

The Barlow Toll Gate was the westernmost tollgate used on the Barlow Road. This tollgate is now reconstructed for tourists at the original site. This tollgate replica is known to be at the exact location because it was built between two maple trees that were planted there by Daniel Parker, an early tollgate keeper. The trees are now very large.

This tollgate was the fifth one used during the years of the Barlow Road. Throughout the years, the gate was at different sites, but only one gate was ever used at a time. For the first two years, Samuel Barlow collected the tolls (fees) at Gate Creek on the eastern end of the Barlow Road. He had not made many road repairs and it was a difficult route, no better than a trail. Since the road was so bad, emigrant P.C. Davis remembered, "Sam Barlow was the most unpopular man in Oregon as far as emigrants of 1846 were concerned." Samuel Barlow gave the road to Oregon's Provisional Government to be made into a free road. It wasn't repaired and became almost impossible to travel. It was then used by others as a toll road until 1919 when it was donated to the state of Oregon.

Operating the Barlow Toll Road was not easy. Many emigrants arrived here hungry and with no money. They refused to pay. Tollkeeper Philip Foster remembered one man who "ran like a turkey" through the gate because he couldn't pay. Often the pioneers had to "pay" with goods or leave IOUs. The ledger of the Barlow and Foster Company showed these unusual payments: J.M. Blanhaby–quilt and $1.50, Sam Tucker–$5.00 and bedspread, and Thomas Donca–coat, pants, and a shirt.

E.W. Conyer's 1852 diary described why it was necessary for the pioneers to have plenty of money:
September 15th: "We are now camped at the foot of the Cascade Mountains, and three miles from the 'Barlow Gate,' where toll is supposed to be taken for the great benefit to be derived by the poor emigrant, worn out by his long trip of 2000 miles across the continent with an ox team, who now has the privilege of paying a few paltry dollars for crossing the last range of mountains laying between him and civilization . . . ."

September 17th: "We find no one here to take toll, and the poor worn-out emigrant is not one bit sorry."

GA1473

The Barlow Road was used for about seventy years. The Barlow Road was no longer needed when the railroad was finished along the Columbia River in 1882, and other alternative routes were opened. A new Mt. Hood highway was built in the 1920s and then improved upon over the years. Today, tourists can travel the Mt. Hood Loop Highway to see parts of the old Barlow Road and think about how difficult the journey was during those early years.

From a July 10, 1853, pioneer letter, these prices were listed as the Barlow Toll Gate prices:

wagon and team	$2.50
man and horse	$ .75
pack animals with packs	$ .25
saddle horses, donkeys, and mules	$ .10
cattle	$ .05
sheep	$ .02 $\frac{1}{2}$

A sign said that widows were free.
Prices varied over the years, depending on the toll keeper.

There was a passageway by the tollgate to let people and animals pass through. The toll keeper would count the animals as they were driven through one at a time. When the toll keeper would reach a 100-count of sheep, for example, he would put a pebble in a box and then start the count over again. After all the sheep passed through, he could count the number of pebbles to determine the total cost, charging about $.02 $\frac{1}{2}$ per sheep.

Some people used the Barlow Road for part of the way and then tried to avoid going through the tollgate and having to pay the toll. If they were caught, they had to pay a penalty of three times the regular price and they also had to pay court costs. One rancher left Summit Meadow on Mt. Hood and drove 3000 sheep down what he thought was the Salmon River to avoid the toll. Instead, he mistakenly drove them down nearby Still Creek. He didn't realize he had joined the Barlow Road. He ended up at the tollgate and had to pay the penalty!

GA1473

Barlow Road Toll Gate Activity

Barlow Road toll keepers would have had to use math every day to determine how much money the emigrants owed them. Pretend you are a toll keeper. Write at least five math story problems that might be situations a toll keeper would have had to calculate on a typical day.

Use the price list on page 84 to help you come up with problems. After you have written the problems, answer them showing all the steps you used to solve the problems. Then, ask a friend to solve the problems. Check them with your answer key.

Example: How much would it cost for this pioneer group to pass through the Barlow Toll Gate: 1 wagon and team, 1 man and horse, 4 cattle, and 6 sheep?

Answer:

1 wagon and team	$2.50 x 1 = $2.50
1 man and horse	.75 x 1 = .75
4 cattle	.05 x 4 = .20
6 sheep	.02 $\frac{1}{2}$ x 6 = .15
Total:	= $3.60

Note: To figure how much this would cost today, due to inflation, multiply the total by 11. Therefore, this $3.60 toll would equal about $39.60 today.

GA1473

Oregon City: End of the Oregon Trail

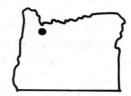

Abernethy Green, Oregon City, OR
17th and Washington Streets
20 minutes from downtown Portland
Clackamas County

After about six months of travel, the emigrants neared the end of the trail, Oregon City. They would cross the Clackamas River and be only about a half day away. If it was late in the season, they would have been met a few days earlier by the relief groups sent out to help the newcomers. Some arrived in good shape, but others arrived needing food, shelter, and clothing. Not far west of Laurel Hill, E. W. Conyers had written in 1852, "Tonight Mrs. Burns made bread from the last of our flour; also, at this meal we consume the last of our meat, and, in fact, we are about out of everything eatable. We live in the hope that there will be plenty for all when we arrive at our destination. My! Oh, my! what a hungry crowd the people of Oregon will have to feed during the coming winter, and the great majority of them have no money to buy with."

Reunions with friends, neighbors, and relatives who had gone to Oregon in earlier years were common every fall and were always occasions for joy. Help was even offered to total strangers. Newcomers were welcome because this added population gave a stronger argument for demanding Congress to grant Oregon statehood and to send more military help.

Peter Burnett wrote about his 1841 journey that he had never lived among such good people as in Oregon. They didn't steal because there was nothing to steal. They didn't drink because there was nothing to drink. They didn't horde because there was nothing to horde. They were all good workers. They had to be or they would have starved.

The *Oregon Spectator*, established in 1846 as the first newspaper west of the Rockies, wrote on September 17, 1846:
  Welcome! ye freeborn yeoman of the soil,
  Right welcome are you to our new made home;
  Here ends your weary pilgrimage and toil,
  You've reached the goal, and need no longer roam.

When they arrived in Oregon City, the emigrants ended their journey at what was called Abernethy Green. (George Abernethy was appointed governor of Oregon's Provisional Government in 1845.) If they arrived on a raft from Fort Vancouver, they landed under what is today I-205 on the east side of the Willamette River and then traveled the short distance to Albernethy Green where they would meet family and friends and prepare to start their new lives.

GA1473

Oregon City was the end of the Oregon Trail since the 40-foot (12-m) drop of the Willamette Falls made it impossible for goods and materials to be shipped farther inland. John McLoughlin had surveyed and laid out the townsite of Oregon City in 1842, and it became the first capital of Oregon. The Provisional and Territorial governments met here from 1843 to 1853 until the capital moved to Salem. Oregon City was a good place for a town because mills could be run from the water power of Willamette Falls. Mills were established to create lumber, flour, woolen cloth, and paper. Overton Johnson said in 1843 as he arrived, ". . . at Oregon City . . . our destination . . . . We found, at the Falls, a small village of about one hundred inhabitants. Lots were laid out on both sides of the river . . . ." Oregon City had the only land office in the West and the only judicial court.

The *Oregon Spectator* described the city the emigrants would find as ". . . a rich and fertile country, and in many places, we might say, bounded with beautiful and luxuriant meadows, encircled with the lofty fir, and interspersed with beautiful groves of oak . . . .

"We are informed that where Oregon City now stands, it was, three years ago, a dense forest of fir and underbrush. The march of improvement has been with gigantic stride. The city is now incorporated with a population of not less than 500 souls, and about eighty houses, to sit: Two churches, two taverns, two blacksmith shops, two cooper shops, two cabinet shops, four tailor shops, one hatter shop, one tannery, three shoe shops, two silversmiths, and a number of other mechanics; four stores, two flouring and two sawmills, and a lath machine . . . .

"We are satisfied that the march of improvement would have been much greater at Oregon City, if nails and paints could have been obtained sufficient to meet the demands of the citizens."

Oregon City became rich from gold that was discovered in California in 1848. Prices of food and lumber went up because of the demand for these products by gold miners. For example, the first load of Oregon-grown apples shipped to California weighed 200 pounds (90 kg) and sold for $500. A later load of Oregon apples of about the same size sold for $2500! Wealthy merchants and prosperous farmers began to replace their log cabins with much better houses. Oregon's currency until 1849 was wheat, but it soon changed to gold dust, and even some gold coins were minted. Women and children were often left behind in Oregon to watch the stores and farms while the male population ran off to the gold fields of California to try to strike it rich.

When the emigrants arrived at Oregon City, ahead of them lay the cold, wet winter and the grim reality of starting a new life in what was then a very primitive area, with only what was left of their wagons. Men often left their families in Oregon City while they searched for a place to call home. Many arrived in October or November. It was often raining, and there might have been snow in the mountains. Pioneers talked about not having feeling in their toes because they were so cold.

Maria P. Belshaw wrote in 1853, ". . . came to the long expected City . . . worst looking place for a City I ever saw . . . ." Mrs. E.J. Goltra described her feelings of her new Oregon land, ". . . do not like Oregon yet, so far." The reality of this first difficult winter must have been very hard on the pioneers. However, one pioneer woman looked back on the early years and claimed, "Never was there a day I wished myself back East to live."

James Nesmith in 1843 wrote, "Then it may be asked, why did such men peril everything–burning their ships behind them, exposing their helpless families to the possibilities of massacres and starvation, braving death–and for what purpose? I am not quite certain that any rational answer will ever be given to that question."

Oregon City Activity

Look at the map of this imaginary region called New Woodland. Imagine that you are a pioneer and have been traveling for five difficult months in a covered wagon and have just arrived at your destination in the region of New Woodland. Leave your wagon and family near the base of Mount Scenic to rest. Go on horseback with some of your friends and explore New Woodland. After looking over the entire region, decide where you and your friends will settle to build your log cabins and start your new jobs.

1. Based on your knowledge of what pioneers would need, put an *X* on the map where you will settle.

2. Write a paragraph explaining why you chose that spot and didn't choose some of the other possible sites. Tell the name of your new town.

3. Then discuss your choice with others so you can explain your thinking and hear the other ideas.

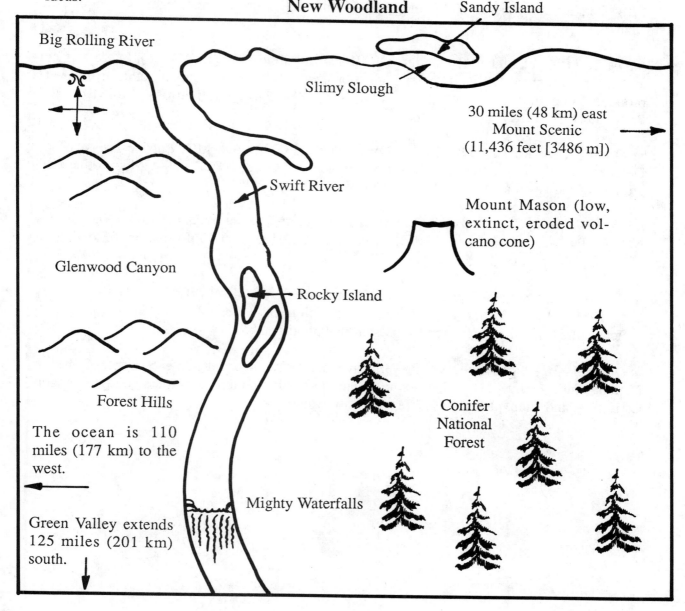

New Woodland

GA1473

Oregon Trail Bibliography and Other Sources

Books:

The Great Platte River Road by Merrill J. Mattes. (Lincoln, NE: University of Nebraska Press, 1969). Classic Oregon Trail book full of descriptions, maps, and pioneer sketches of emigration along the Platte River–from Independence to Fort Laramie

Historic Sites Along the Oregon Trail by Aubrey L. Haines. (St. Louis, MO: Patrice Press, 1981). Excellent guidebook for finding 394 sites as one travels the trail today

Most of the Oregon Trail by Gregory M. Franzwa. (Gerald, MO: Patrice Press, 1982). Overview information on the trail plus extremely detailed maps of the Oregon Trail as it currently crosses the United States (They have merchandise and books available through their catalog: 1810 West Grant Rd., Suite 108, Tucson, AZ 85745.)

National Geographic Magazine, "Life and Death on the Oregon Trail–The Itch to Move West," by Boyd Gibbons. (Washington, DC: National Geographic Society, August 1986, Volume 170). Detailed information and photographs of the emigrant trails to Oregon, California, and Utah

Oregon Trail by Rick Steber. (Prineville, OR: Bonanza Publications, Ltd., 1986). Interesting collection of short stories of the Oregon Trail. Bonanza Publications has many other frontier and pioneer books and tapes for adults and children (Bonanza Publications, Ltd., Box 204, Prineville, OR 97754).

The Oregon Trail Revisited by Gregory M. Franzwa. (St. Louis, MO: Patrice Press, 1988). Detailed guidebook for finding sites as one travels the Oregon Trail today. Many other emigrant books are available through Patrice Press.

Oregon Trail, Voyage of Discovery–The Story Behind the Scenery by Dan Murphy. (Las Vegas, NV: KC Publications, Inc., 1991). Lovely colored photographs and information, following the trail from Missouri to Oregon

The Oregon Trail–Yesterday & Today by William E. Hill. (Caldwell, ID: The Caxton Printers, Ltd., 1986). History of the Oregon Trail, maps, pioneer guidebooks and diaries, plus early sketches of sites with comparisons to present-day photographs

The Overland Migrations by David Sievert Lavender. (Washington, D.C.: U.S. Dept. of Interior, National Park Service, 1980). Details information and photographs of settlers going to Oregon, California, and Utah, plus pioneer life and historic sites

The Pioneers by Editors of Time-Life Books with text by Huston Hora. (Chicago, IL: Time-Life Books, Inc., 1974). Extremely complete book with information on the reasons for the emigrations, missionaries, the journeys, settlements, Mormons, sodbusters

Trails West by Special Publications Division. (Washington, D.C.: National Geographic Society, 1979). Information and photographs on these trails west: Oregon, Santa Fe, Mormon, California, Gila, and Bozeman

Women's Diaries of the Westward Journey by Lillian Schlissel. (New York, NY: Schocken Books, 1982). Information on families on the trails plus emigrant diaries of four women: Lydia A. Rudd, Amelia S. Knight, Catherine Haun, and Jane G. Tourtillott

Sources That Have Good Information on the Sager Family:

Cobblestone Magazine by editors and guest authors. (Peterborough, NH: Cobblestone Publishing, Inc., December 1981, Volume 2). This history magazine for young people covers a different theme for each issue. This issue is devoted entirely to the Oregon Trail with information geared to students. Back issues are available.

Conversations with Pioneer Women (The Lockley Files) compiled and edited by Mike Helm. (Eugene, OR: Rainy Day Press, 1981). Fred Lockley was an Oregon pioneer newspaperman. He conducted over 10,000 interviews with all segments of frontier settlers. This book is a fascinating collection of interviews of pioneer women. Especially interesting are the interviews with Elizabeth and Matilda Sager.

Seven for Oregon by Cornelia Shields. (Dayton, WA: Green Springs Press, 1986). The novel is based on the Sager Family's true adventures on the Oregon Trail.

Stout-Hearted Seven by Neta Lohnes Frazier. (Seattle, WA: Pacific Northwest National Parks & Forests Association, 1984). True story of the Sager children

GA1473

Other Sources for Studying the Oregon Trail:

Oregon-California Trails Association

- P.O. Box 1019, Independence, MO 64051-0519, Phone and FAX (812) 252-2276
- This large national organization includes the quarterly publication of the *Overland Journal*, regional newsletters, national and local conventions, tours, and trail preservation.
- OCTA has a catalog available for maps, trail merchandise, books, back issues of the journal, and a special section for children.

Pioneers–A Simulation of Decision-Making on a Wagon Train

- By John Wesley (Lakeside, CA: Interact Company, 1974)
- This company publishes many simulations that stress cooperative learning and problem solving. *Pioneers* has been their best-seller for years! Students draw names for pioneer identities, select supplies for their wagons, write journal entries, and are challenged to make decisions that will decide their fate on the "Hacker Trail."
- A catalog is available from Interact, P.O. Box 997-Y89, Lakeside, CA 92040, Phone: (619) 448-1474.

Made in Oregon–This is a chain of stores and catalog that sell products promoting the Oregon Trail, such as wooden covered wagons, maps, T-shirts, Oregon Trail dust, dolls, books, jewelry, tote bags, candy, tapes of pioneer music, buffalo chips, soap. Made in Oregon, P.O. Box 3458, Portland, OR 97208-3458, (800) 828-9673.

Touch the Past sponsored by the St. Joseph Museum with Esther Kreek. (St. Joseph, MO: St. Joseph Museum, 1984) Includes a fictionalized diary of the trip west with printed music and a tape of songs that would have been sung during Oregon Trail days. Available from St. Joseph Museum, 11th & Charles, St. Joseph, MO 64501.

Wagon Train 1848–This Oregon Trail computer software introduces students to the westward movement through interactive, collaborative problem-solving. Students try to survive the trek, making decisions such as what to do if someone gets sick, which way to go if the trail divides, and where to hunt for food. Available from MECC, 6160 Summit Drive N., Minneapolis, MN 55430, Phone (800) 685-6322.

Every effort has been made, at the time of publication, to insure the accuracy of the information included in this book. We cannot guarantee, however, that the agencies and organizations we have mentioned will continue to operate or to maintain these current locations indefinitely.